To my terri'... I love so Riley. —Ronna

Somewhere Out There

My Experience of Adoption and the
Search for Understanding

By
Ronna Quimby Huckaby

Wild Horse Press
www.wildhorsepress.com

Dedicated to my loving parents:

Evert Ronald Quimby
&
Frances Johnson Quimby

A special dedication to Billy, my husband, who encouraged me to start on this special journey.

ISBN-10 0-9814903-5-2   ISBN-13 978-0-9814903-5-9

All Inquiries regarding this book should be addressed to
Wild Horse Press
P.O. Box 3 • Walnut Springs, TX 76690
254-797-2629
E-Mail wildhorsepress@att.net
www.WildHorsePress.com

Acknowledgments

The first time I heard the song "Somewhere Out There" I quickly related to the words. It summed up how I felt about being adopted…that somewhere out there was the woman who gave birth to me. Whenever a national news story would happen, I would think about how she was hearing the story too. We shared the same moon and stars each night. So I am grateful for the song that gave me the inspiration to write.

In 1994, I started making notes. And after meeting my now, husband, Billy, who was a "real" writer, I started getting more serious about formalizing my ideas. I wish to express my gratitude to him for jump-starting this endeavor. Billy, I appreciate your knowledge of book publishing and desire to help me succeed. Thank you for making me laugh along the way. I love you so very much.

Also, I am especially grateful to our friends Dan Malone and Kathryn Jones, award winning journalists- whose guidance and editing have given me confidence and strength to produce a finished copy. I am humbled by your words of encouragement, grateful for your help, and most of all thankful for your friendship.

To Elizabeth "Betsy" Wilson Lockhart Blowers, her husband Ray, Alix and Wink Lockhart, Julie Watson, Riley Harvill and the entire Auld Family, my sincere thanks for loving me, accepting me, and helping me fill in the blanks. My love and thanks to all my family.

I must also thank a few dear friends: Sandy Lambert Page and Judith Alexander Priest. Sandy and I have been friends since we were five years old. It amazes me that all these years we have been so close, even when our paths didn't cross on a daily basis. I am so grateful and lucky to have someone who truly defines the meaning of "true friendship." Also, Judith is someone who taught me about being real. She gave me a safe haven of friendship where I could speak my mind and share my inner thoughts—as crazy as they might have been at times—still knowing that afterwards, she would still love me and be there for me.

Others who have played a vital role in my search are Bonnie Solecki and Rebekah Oursler. I thank both of these ladies for their part, Bonnie for her determination to help me uncover the truth and Rebekah for helping me find the courage to take the next step in the process.

My thanks to the folks associated with Homestead Maternity Home Yahoo Group as well as other adoptees. To adoptees and birthmothers—those who are enjoying their reunions and to those who are still searching and waiting. I thank you and wish you peace and contentment on this road of life.

And lastly and most important, I must thank the leading characters in this book and in my life: my parents, two remarkable individuals, Frances and Evert Quimby. I am PROUD to be your daughter and cherish every memory I have of our life. When I think of honest heroes, I think of my father. A quiet man, although not educated, he made a tremendous impact on this world through his honesty and hard work. And when I think of fun-loving women, I think of my mother, a gentle, humble soul who could always make me laugh, whose spirit and faith never waivered. Their love and devotion to me throughout my life is irreplaceable. They believed in me like no other. I thank them and dedicate this book to them.

Ronna

Table of Contents

Somewhere out there
beneath the pale moonlight,
Someone's thinking of me and loving me tonight.

Somewhere out there someone's saying a prayer
That we'll find one another
in that big somewhere out there.
And even though I know how very far apart we are,
It helps to think we might be wishin' on the same bright
star.
And when the night wind starts to sing a lonesome lullaby,
It helps to think we're sleeping underneath the same big
sky.

Somewhere out there if love can see us through,
Then we'll be together, somewhere out there,
Out where dreams come true.

From "Somewhere Out There," Lyrics by
James Horner, Barry Mann, and Cynthia Weil

Introduction: The Journey Begins

Fort Worth, Texas 1999

As I embarked on the journey before me, I thought of the millions of others who faced this same trip or who traveled down this same road. Ironically, it is a road well traveled; yet I felt like I was headed into uncharted territory--ready to claim the land for all adoptees. I will figure it out and map out the course and that will be that. I will plant the proverbial flag in virgin soil, stating that I have arrived. Case closed.

However, it is not that simple. Even though countless others have made this journey, today I am alone on this trail. For this is an individual task and my only competition is myself, or shall I say the *fear* of my "self." I am setting out on a course, not knowing the ending or even if there is an ending. I wonder if I am stepping on to a road that leads nowhere. At the end of the road will I find what I am searching for? Do I even know what that is? The song "Somewhere Out There" refers to "Out there where dreams come true." What are my dreams? Will they come true? Nonetheless, this journey is a part of life, part of *my* life anyway, my life as an adopted child…to discover what is true.

I read an article in the local paper about a story of the pros and cons of open adoption records. There was one quote from someone who had several things to

say about adoptees and one's search for self. Although
I cannot remember the remark verbatim, it was
something like this: "Quit blaming your bad experiences
and/or choices on being adopted."
　　This book is not about blame. It is about belonging.

　　For over a decade, I have counseled survivors of
domestic violence. I have worked with many clients who
were dealing with issues such as depression, low self-
esteem, and victimization. Each individual client would
report to me basically the same story. Each one felt
confused, alone, crazy and isolated. Consequently,
when I would talk about the cycle of violence, and the
common dynamics of the relationship, their eyes would
widen as they asked, "How did you know?" They
appeared amazed that I knew something "no one else
had known" as if I were a mouse in the corner and had
seen into their world. This seemed to bring them some
comfort, comfort that it was not in their imaginations but
feelings based on actual facts. Someone had confirmed
it for them. They were not alone.
　　Common themes run through our parallel lives.
When faced with fear and uncertainty, it is very
reassuring to know you are not alone and others have
had similar feelings. Often we can find comfort by just
knowing we are not the only person in this situation,
whatever it may be. That is why support groups are so
helpful. It helps alleviate the "I'm the only one who ever
felt like this" feelings of isolation that can lead to
negative self-talk and hopelessness. Realizing that we are

not the only one who is or has experienced something validates our feelings.

Maybe you are not an adopted child. Maybe you are a birth parent or adoptive parent, or just an interested party. Nonetheless, we all search for understanding of our unique worlds. Often that search begins with questions of "why?"

Many times our "why's" are never answered. What do we do then? The questions linger. The world goes on, we go on. We really do not have any other choice. We must "accept the things we cannot change." We survive.

Maybe we do find some answers. But do the answers bring understanding? Can they always bring understanding? Isn't it the understanding that we are really seeking? There is a fine line between *finding the answer to our questions "why?"* and *understanding.*

Often we are given an answer to the complex question. "Why did the mother drive her children into a lake and drown them?" The answer: because she was depressed and felt overwhelmed. But does that answer bring us comfort and the ability to say "OK, I understand"? We have answers but no understanding.

My search for answers about my adoption and my search for understanding are my story.

This was not even a journey that I anticipated ever taking. There were not any sleepless nights pondering the question, "Should I search or shouldn't I?" It just happened. Even now, looking back, I cannot remember the catalyst that started my search. My husband, who is a writer, took interest in my being adopted. And being the journalist, he did some brief research on the subject, gave me some articles that he found on adoption, and then for me it all just sort of started.

My experience is unique to me. There are millions of others out there with stories. I do not claim to have all the answers for other adoptees or those involved in the process of adoption. However, because I am adopted, I am an expert on <u>my</u> experience. And as I look over the miles I have covered, I see common themes that surface in my life. In talking with other adoptees, I see those same themes surface. Sometimes the themes may not float to the surface in an obvious way, but I am certain that they are there. Recognizing and understanding some of these themes may lead to a greater level of understanding. They may not answer the questions, but it may be a start. As for me the answers and understanding are . . . somewhere out there.

Chapter 1
Baby Girl Lamb

I am Ronna. I am an adopted child. I was adopted when I was six days old. I was raised in a small, rural North Texas town. My childhood left me with many wonderful memories of life with my adoptive parents, Frances and Evert Quimby.

1949

At the age of twenty-four, Frances Johnson found herself knee deep in three feet of snow as she looked around her new world. She was living in Minneapolis, Minnesota. She left her hometown in Texas to explore the world. And there she was, far from home and ready to see what the world had to offer. Her travels had taken her to Little Rock, Arkansas, Boulder, Colorado, and eventually she headed north to Minnesota. Minneapolis was a far cry from Bowie, Texas, a small rural town in North Texas. As the daughter of a cotton farmer, sister to five brothers and two sisters, she was stuck somewhere in the middle. A middle child had its difficulties, but Frances was giving and adventurous.

But now she was in Minnesota where the winters are cold. She recounted the story of her daily activities.

"I was working as a waitress at Lee's Broiler," Frances said. "Lee's was a really nice restaurant, a local chain. My best friend, Ollie, and I lived together in the city and would stop off for breakfast each morning at a local diner."

The diner was Ruth's Café. Almost everyday, Frances and Ollie would see two young men at the diner. The men had just finished the midnight shift at the local tractor factory and frequently would stop by the diner to grab a bite to eat before heading home for a much-needed rest.

This particular morning, Al, the outspoken male of the duo, asked if they could join the two ladies. Ollie gave the go ahead for the two men to share the booth. Frances was somewhat unsure about this. She described Al as a "big mouth, always popping off." But that other guy, the quiet one, always was grinning.

"He was really cute!" Frances recalled. "He had a

Frances at 14

big curl hanging on his forehead." She later found out his sister-in-law had given him a perm.

"They came over, acting like they wanted to sit down and I was scared to death that Al was going to sit by me. Somehow, I don't know if I made eyes at Evert or what, but he sat by me." Frances continued. It was an answer to her secret prayer, in more ways than she expected.

His name was Evert Ronald Quimby. He was about five foot, eight inches, and thin, with a crooked smile, dark hair, and hazel eyes. He didn't say much but the chemistry was unmistakable, like a spark igniting the soul of the little gal from Texas. Evert's cowlick gave him a rugged look, sort of a Marlon Brando type, mischievous, rugged, yet soft on the inside.

Evert was born and raised in Hines, Minnesota, located in the northeastern part of the state. Apart from the years he spent in the Navy, he had always called the land of 10,000 lakes home. He was the ninth of ten children — five girls, five boys. He had never seen a girl quite like Frances. He wasn't sure what was different. Maybe it was her pretty blue eyes or that sweet Texas drawl. When he was asked if he had ever been in love before, he said laughingly, "No, I'd never do that. Just one girl."

It was a wonderful way for the four to start a day, or end a day for that matter. And it would become a daily ritual. They would meet for early morning coffee for weeks to come.

Evert in 1945

Soon Evert and Frances would spend more than their mornings together. He called her Frannie and was quickly falling in love. He had never really been in love before but he was sure of his feelings now. Frannie had loved and lost. The pain was still there. As a result, she was cautious.

They began dating in the fall, as winter approached, fear began to set in for young Frances.

"He was rushing things and I wasn't ready," she said. "He wanted to get serious so I thought I'd just go home for a while." Frances went back to Texas, to her family's farm, where life was simple, to think things through. She wanted the peace and quiet of the countryside. However, it wasn't exactly the experience she was hoping for. "I was miserable," she said. "I didn't have a car, I wanted to get a job but didn't. I was really lonely."

Evert, who could be described as the strong, silent type remembers he was lonely as well. He said his heart was broken.

"I wrote letters to her and that's something I just don't do." Evert confessed.

"Oh, he wanted to come to Texas and see me," Frances interjected. "But I didn't want him to."

Frances had had enough of "thinking things through." She decided to head north. Without calling ahead to tell him she was coming, Frances boarded a train back to Minnesota.

Like a scene from some old black-and-white romantic movie, she arrived at the train station and briskly walked to the diner. She said she just knew he would be there. It was cold, but that didn't slow her pace as she headed to the little diner where it had all started.

Uncertain of how the reunion would go, her insides felt full of butterflies. Would Evert be happy to see her? Would he be sitting with someone new?

I asked her why she didn't tell anyone she was coming. "I knew I'd find him or he'd find me," she said.

She stood outside the diner, carrying her small suitcase. Peering through the window, she saw him sitting in a booth with a few of his buddies. They were drinking coffee and laughing. Evert walked up to the counter to talk with the cook.

She stepped inside the door and the little bell which hung on the door knob gave a little jingle.

"I looked at the door and there stood Frannie. I thought, 'damn, what's going on here?" He couldn't believe his eyes.

Without hesitation, he ran to her. He picked her up in his arms and slung her around with delight. She had come back to him. It was the beginning of spring and of something wonderful.

Evert had been living with his brother in a suburb of Minneapolis and soon moved into the city from his brother's house.

"I was so broke I couldn't pay attention. But I would walk over to Frannie's apartment, pick her up and we'd just walk around the city." Evert recalled. He was making less than a dollar an hour. But in his heart, he wanted to get married. So his plan began. He went and bought a ring.

How was he going to pay for this, I asked? Together, he and Frances replied in unison "Credit." Frances still had the receipt for her ring; A lovely three-quarter carat diamond, a symbol of his love for her.

"I went to her place and pulled the ring out of my pocket and simply said 'Will you marry me'?"

"Well, I sure want that ring," Frances said.

That was a "yes." He put the ring on her finger and she says she didn't take it off for a very long time. "I still cherish this ring and only take it off when absolutely necessary," Frances said.

Mr. & Mrs. Evert Quimby
November 4, 1950

They were married on November 4, 1950, in a very small ceremony. Ollie and Evert's brother Don stood as witnesses. It was snowing, of course.

The Quimbys lived in Minneapolis for seven years. They made a lovely couple. Evert drove a cab and Frances was a wonderful housewife. They had a loving home. Lots of Evert's family, four brothers and five sisters, to be exact and lots of friends filled their days, but something was missing: A baby. Having both come from large families, they wanted a family of their own.

So they began trying to conceive. Years passed and Frances was not pregnant. They consulted with doctors, underwent a battery of tests, and prayed to God to "Please give us a baby." Frances was in her mid-thirties and knew time was running out.

All the tests proved to be inconclusive. The doctors could not find a medical reason why the loving couple could not conceive.

In 1957, they moved to Texas. Evert was tired of the cold weather and wanted to see what the Lone Star State had to offer. They bought a small trailer house on Mill Street in Bowie, northwest of Dallas. He began working in the oil field as a roughneck and Frances worked at home. She longed for a child.

Evert Arrives in Texas

The minister from their church suggested they consider adoption. It had crossed their minds on a few occasions but it seemed too complicated, too expensive.

"We were good money managers but the oilfield was so unpredictable," Evert recalls. "I was making about $1.35 an hour. I would have steady work for a few months, then the rig would be down and I might be off for a month. But we wanted a baby."

Frances wanted a baby so badly that she would often interpret any possible symptom—late period, nausea, or stomach pains—as possibly being pregnant. It is no secret how much Frances wanted a baby. And the reality that she was not expecting was very disappointing.

Their pastor gave them material on a nearby home for unwed mothers. In April of 1961, they had their first interview with the social worker from Homestead Maternity Home.

Homestead Maternity Home

Homestead Maternity Home was located in Fort Worth, Texas. It was a non-profit, charitable corporation that opened in 1957. Actually it is unclear the exact dates of operation. It was licensed in October of 1958 however it appears that it opened 1954-1955. It was managed by a board of directors that included several doctors, a nurse, a minister, an attorney, and other prominent citizens. The first Executive Director was Mrs. W. W. Slaughter until a retired Baptist minister, Dr. T. E. Durham took over. Dr. Durham was previously on the board and was involved with Homestead from the day it opened until the facility closed. A house mother stayed at the home with the girls. It could house up to eighty pregnant girls. The girls could enter the home any time during their pregnancy, but the home preferred that they arrive

during their fourth or fifth month. The brochure that
Evert and Frances received stated that a girl "may desire
to enter earlier to conceal her condition." The decision
to give up the baby for adoption had to have already
been made. One birthmom, Mary, said that the home
was not "too different from the sorority house-except it
wasn't as fancy and we all had big bellies." Up until the
last month of pregnancy, the girls had chores' to do
such as cooking and cleaning. They were required to

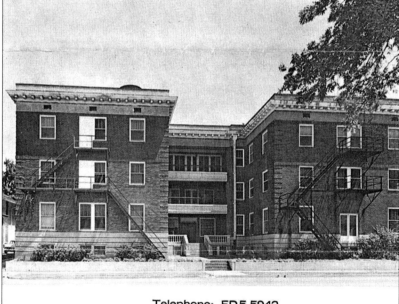

The Homestead Maternity Home

1250 West Rosedale Avenue
FORT WORTH, TEXAS

Telephone: ED 5-5942
ED 6-7905
ED 2-2527
Nite Number: ED 6-7905
DR. T. E. DURHAM, B.A., Th.M., Ph.D.
Executive Director

do their own laundry and keep their rooms tidy. No formal counseling was provided. Birthmothers report that they were told that they were doing the right thing for their babies and that they would go on with their lives and would forget the whole experience. All records bore an assumed name of the woman, with her real identity known only to the office personnel. The assumed last name would start with the same letter as the unwed mother's real last name. For a girl whose name was Smith might have the assumed name of Sanders. The original birth certificate would display the actual name, as well as the Certificate of Adoption that would be finalized six months later.

However once the adoption was finalized the birth certificate was amended and listed the adoptive parents as the "original" parents of the child.

At Homestead, many girls would even change the spelling of their real name or other information because of fear and shame.

The Home required prospective parents to complete a seven-page application, provide reference letters, and submit to individual interviews. The waiting period varied. All attempts were made to "match" the natural mother with the adoptive mother in nationality, height, coloring, and so forth. The same was true for the birth father and adoptive father.

According to letters written in 1961 from the supervisor of social work at Homestead, minimum qualifications for adoptive parenthood were:

1. Couples must be under forty years of age.
2. They must be in good health.
3. A couple must have an income sufficient for adequate family living. Preference was given to couples with annual incomes of $5,000.
4. Couples had to present proof of recent sterility tests before an application could be approved.
5. Couples were to be married for at least three years if it was the first marriage and five years if it was the second marriage of either party.

Home visits were conducted and the couple had to present a copy of their marriage certificate.

The Quimbys met all the requirements and sent an application to Homestead. On August 31, 1961, they received word that their first interview would take place in September. This would not be a quick process. Several letters were written over the next few years inquiring about the savings plan that was required to make the Quimbys eligible. In a letter dated December 19, 1962, a social worker wrote:

> . . . *please let me know how much you have saved to this point, so that I might know better when you could be considered for a baby.*

Frances and Evert finally reached a point in their savings where they were able to make a formal application for an infant to be placed in their care. Now they would just have to wait.

1963

At 1:30 in the afternoon on January 24, 1963 the telephone rang in the small blue trailer on Mill Street, in Bowie, Texas. Without anticipation of what was about to happen, Frances quickly answered.

"Hello."

"Mrs. Quimby?" the voice asked.

"Yes," replied Frances.

"We have a little girl for you," the voice on the other said.

Trailer - Bowie, Texas

"My first question was 'when can we pick her up'" Frances later recalled. "They told me we had to wait until the baby was six days old." The baby was born on Tuesday, January 22. Six days would be Sunday, which meant she and Evert would have to wait until Monday.

"I didn't think I would live through the weekend," she said, laughing. "On Sunday, we went to church but I don't even remember being there." During the phone call, the social worker shared some basic information about the baby's biological parents.

Mother: age 23, single. 5'2 ½ ", 110 pounds. 2 years college. Both parents had college degrees. Scotch-Irish. Blonde hair, green eyes. Worked as a flight attendant "airline hostess".

Father: young man, Anglo, single, 5'6", 150 pounds, High School Education. Brown hair, green eyes, dark complexion. Worked at a beach hotel as recreation director.

This is the information that had been reported from the pregnant woman when she entered into Homestead.

Frances kept the news to herself until Evert came home from work. When he opened the door he found a sign on the door: *"Congratulations Daddy!"*

"We didn't tell anyone," Evert said.

"I didn't want to get everyone's hopes up, so we didn't tell anyone," Frances said — except the banker.

The social worker from Homestead told Frances they needed to bring a check for $750 — more than this oil-field worker and housewife had at their immediate disposal.

As Evert recalled the memory, tears welled in his eyes. "I used to buy groceries at a local grocery store and charge them and I always paid my bill. Well, the owner sold the store and he became a banker. I went down to the bank on Friday morning and sat at his desk. I told him what I wanted. I told him what it was for. I told him 'I don't have any collateral, I owe on a '59 Ford, a trailer house and the lot it sits on but I need this money.' He didn't say a word, turned the forms towards me and he just said 'Sign right here.'"

On Sunday afternoon, the day before the trip to pick up their new daughter, Frances asked her sister Pauline if she could fix her hair. Pauline was a hairdresser and worked at a local salon. Frances also invited her mother and other sister, Peb. She couldn't keep it in any longer. Frances recalled that there was not a dry eye in the beauty shop all afternoon. Just as someone would gain their composure, someone else would start back up. It was a tag team of cries of joy.

When Monday morning finally came, Frances and Evert loaded up their Ford and started out for Fort Worth, some 80 miles southeast. It was a cold day in January of 1963. Both sat in silence during the drive, filled with anticipation of the changes that were about to happen in their lives.

"We were both really quiet, but we were really smiling," Evert recalled.

"I was so nervous," Frances said. "Then out of nowhere, a huge, beautiful Monarch butterfly lit on the hood of the car. It traveled with us for miles. I knew then that everything was going to be OK. It was my sign --where else would a butterfly come from in the dead of winter, snow on the ground, except from Heaven"?

Again, with tears in his eyes, Evert said, "We got to the agency and shortly a nurse came over from Harris Hospital with the baby all wrapped up in a little pink blanket."

Frances' legs were shaking. Evert looked at the nurse and pointed to his wife. The nurse handed the bundle to her.

Frances told me, "I can remember sitting down and lifting up the blanket and seeing your face for the first time. It was the most beautiful thing I had ever seen. I just fell over you and cried."

The paperwork from the adoption agency referred to the child as "baby girl Lamb." Evert and Frances agreed that this child was a precious lamb.

In 1999—36 years later, the three of us sat around the kitchen table and as my parents recalled that day so long ago, we all cried. It was a moment that I would cherish for all my days.

"You were wrapped in a little pink blanket. I checked the diaper I bet a hundred times. I was so anxious to change your diaper for the first time," Frances said.

For my parents it was a miracle. They pulled in the driveway of their small home on Mill Street. Only the few family members knew that they were picking up a new member of the family. They walked into the house, holding their new baby daughter, oblivious to the world outside. This was a new journey, full of potential, excitement, and never-ending joy. They were right about that! They left that morning a happy couple and returned as a happy family.

The neighbor called. Evert told them they should walk over and see what they had. The neighbor said "Oh, I bet you got a new puppy."

"Come see for yourself" boasted the proud new daddy.

Well, it wasn't a puppy, and it still wasn't "house broken." Frances continued to check the diaper.

A few family members soon arrived to share in the joy of the newest member of the family. Frances's sister, Pauline Harvill, her husband Bert and sons Riley, age seven and Kevin, age four.

When Pauline was at work, she would bring Kevin for Frances to babysit. Frances called Kevin "her boy." Being Frances' "little boy", Kevin wasn't quite sure if he was as excited as everyone else about this new kid on the block. What would that do to his daily routine with his Aunt Frances. What was the fuss all about? She was awfully little. She couldn't play outside, catch a ball or ride a bike. He didn't know if this was going to work or not. But it wasn't long before Kevin took a shine to the new little one. Kevin and I have shared a very special relationship throughout the years. He has been more like a brother to me than a cousin. We have shared many secrets, tears and laughs. But when you look at the pictures from my arrival on the scene, you can easily see that he is just not sure how things would turn out.

Riley recalls that no other relatives were there on that first day. It was very small and precious gathering. And although no specific details can be remembered, he said he does remember how happy everyone felt.

When asked if my being adopted was ever a conversation among family members, he reports that he never felt like I was any different than any other cousin or member of the family. He remembers that often he, Kevin and I would talk about who my birthparents were and they would fantasize that my father must be a Dallas Cowboy.

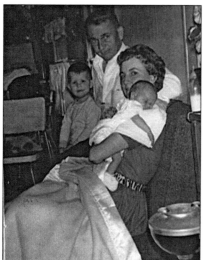 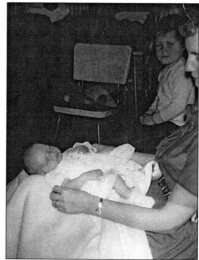

Kevin, new daddy Evert, new mommie Frances and baby Ronna **Six days old - Kevin is just not sure about her.**

Chapter 2
I Am Special

My name is Ronna Sue Quimby. *Ronna* is after my dad, whose middle name is Ronald. Mama said she heard it in a movie once and thought it would be the perfect name. *Sue* is after two people. I have an Aunt Sue, married to my mother's brother, Troy. Also, my mother helped take care of a young woman, 20, who was crippled from polio. Her name was Sue and her mama described her as an angel. My mama thought it was only fitting that her angel was named *Sue* as well.

Ronna - Age 3

The Scare 1965 . . .

In 1965, the Quimby's were very happy. They had moved from the little blue trailer on Mill Street into a 3 bedroom house on Wilbarger Street. The lovely house had a big yard for Ronna to play. Frances had a lovely flower garden and a wonderful vegetable garden. They would spend many hours outside enjoying the sun and new yard.

In June while watching Ronna play in the yard, she noticed that Ronna would run and play and then next thing she would see Ronna sitting still, sometimes laying on the ground. She was not crying and sometimes would even be singing so she wasn't too concerned at the moment. Later that night during Ronna's bath, Frances felt a large mass in her lower belly. Frances quickly called for Evert to come to verify the discovery. Yes, it was not her imagination. There was something there. What could be the problem with the baby that they had waited to have for so long? Morning could not come quick enough so they could take Ronna to the doctor.

After a sleepless night, morning finally came and they took her to the doctor. The doctor confirmed that there was definitely something there and quickly called a pediatric surgeon in Wichita Falls. The Quimbys made the 50 mile journey.

The initial diagnosis was Wilms Tumor. Wilms Tumor is a rare kidney cancer that primarily affects children. Surgery would be performed the next day. Frances, Evert and the whole family were worried sick.

After surgery was complete, the good news was delivered that it was not Wilms tumor. However, it was not completely a good report. Once into the surgery, the doctors found that the left ovary and fallopian tube were twisted around the right tube and ovary. There were several cysts like growths and without a pathologist, it was decided to remove both ovaries and tubes. Ronna would never be able to have her own biological children.

I remember when I was very young, maybe six or seven, while taking a bath; my mother came into the bathroom and told me about the scar on my belly. And even though I don't remember her exact words, I do remember her telling me that I was very special and that I would be able to adopt children one day just like she had done. She told me that God had a very special plan for me.

My childhood was filled with laughter and precious memories. Our family as well as our extended family were very close. All but two of my mother's brothers lived in Bowie, so holidays as well as Saturdays were usually spent together.

Every Saturday night, family members would gather at my grandfather's house. My grandmother, Orlie

Quimby Family - Age 4

Johnson, died when I was only two. My grandfather sold the farm and moved to town a few years later. I can remember so many things about his house on Jefferson Street in Bowie. It had a large front porch and a large screened-in back porch, with the perfect stoops to play Army (when the boy cousins were in charge) and café-waitress and customers (when the girl cousins were in charge).

A fond memory of my grandfather's house was the goodies I would find in his kitchen. In his kitchen he had a Formica table where he kept chips, loaves of bread and all kinds of treats. He kept his leftover biscuits in a coffee can. That coffee can could always be found on the grey table top. They always tasted so good. So much that I asked my mama to put our leftover biscuits in a coffee can. She did, but they never had the same flavor as Grandpa's.

Another food that always brings back childhood memories of my grandfather is candied orange slices and those orange colored, peanut shaped, foam-style candy. Still don't know what those things were but evidently, my grandfather had a sweet tooth for them.

Saturday nights at Grandpa's were filled with the women chatting about children, church, and recipes while the men often played dominoes. The children played outside. My cousin Kevin was my hero. If he was around, I knew I was going to have fun. My cousin Glenn would often be there as well as we three would play army or sit around talking about how we were going to form a club and charge dues and make lots of money. I was always voted the secretary. Since I was only eight years old, that position was quite an honor.

When I was four, my mother's brother Paul went through a divorce. He was left to care for four children: Gayle, about fourteen; twin girls Jan and Ann, eight years old; and Darrell, who was six. Paul could not work and care for the children, so until he could get on his feet, his sisters stepped in to help.

Ann Johnson

Peb, Frances' oldest sister still had two teenage girls at home so Gayle went to live with her. Pauline (a twin to Paul) had two sons, Kevin, who was nine, and Riley, fourteen, so she took Darrell. Frances took the twins. I now had two slightly older sisters.

The new additions to my family strained my father financially. My mother worked at home, so the increase in the expenses was quite costly for this single-income family.

Jan Johnson

But there were no complaints and my parents welcomed the twins as if they were their very own.

Shortly before Ann and Jan came to live with us, my parents were entertaining the idea of trying to adopt a second child. We had moved from the small trailer when I was two and into a larger house to hold a larger family. But when the twins came, Mom and Dad knew that this could be a permanent situation. So they put the adoption plans on hold.

Ann and Jan were in second grade when they lived with us. Ann had dark brown hair, Jan was blonde. Mama and Daddy worked hard to make them feel like they were part of the family. Mama would make us all three matching dresses. She would spend time with each of us individually.

I have a few memories of playing dress up and house. Jan would be the mother, I would be the child and Ann always wanted to be the dog. We were family.

Christmas morning in matching gowns Mama made for us.

However, after a year, Paul moved to Keller, Texas, where he had a secure job and was ready for his family to reunite. The twins left to return to their father. It was once again just the three of us, Mama, Daddy and me.

Shortly after that I started kindergarten. A few years later, when I was about nine the topic of adopting another child again came up. My mother and I talked about it often. We both talked about a baby brother. We even named him, Chad Evert Quimby. My mother and I were huge fans of the TV show *Medical Center* starring Chad Everett. I am not sure what happened with the idea of another child. I do not remember a conversation that said they would not be adopting. I never thought to ask. My mother was now over forty and that may have been an influencing factor. However, I enjoyed being an only child, my mother's dream angel and my daddy's little girl.

Childhood was a wonderful time for me. I have so many vivid memories. When I started first grade, I had a *Family Affair* lunchbox. I was so excited. I would re-arrange my pencil box with my fat pencils, and crayons and thumb through my Big Chief tablet. Mama even would fix my lunch and let me "practice" carrying my lunch to school. I remember the week before I started school, walking out to the curb with my lunchbox full of fried chicken, grapes, and grape Kool-ade. I sat on the curb and enjoyed every bite. Even today, I will eat a grape that has that same taste as the ones I enjoyed on the curb so many years ago.

I always had great dolls, a Barbie house, and a beautiful bedroom. My first Barbie house was three cardboard boxes stacked on top of each other. Mama cut out windows and then covered them with plastic wrap to resemble glass. She even took a few twigs and glued them across the window to look like tree branches outside. Years later I got a "store bought" Barbie house and it just wasn't as fun. My bedroom was always red—red and white checks, or red and white polka dots. My ceiling had glow in the dark stars that formed the

Big Dipper and other starry areas. My childhood friend, Jarae Shelton Scruggs recalls "I remember thinking that you had the coolest room and how lucky you were." My mama was so creative, making life fun and exciting each day. My dolls and I had matching dresses that my mother would sew. She built me a tree house and was always willing to take time to teach me and spend quality

Wearing my Jr. Airline Hostess jumper in the 3rd grade.

time with me. Anyone that spent anytime with my mama realized quickly how funny she was…she loved to play jokes and be silly. She would do something funny and then she would "snicker".

When I was young and playing house was my favorite pastime, mama would always play along. On Saturday mornings, we would play beauty shop. I would come to the kitchen with my dolls in the buggy and tell her I was there for my appointment. I would then climb on the cabinet, lay my head over the sink and she would wash my hair. We would make "small talk" about *my* children and *my* husband (I would usually be *married* to a current celebrity. Looking back I can remember being linked to the likes of James Arness from *Gunsmoke,* Roy Clark from *Hee Haw* (who knew he was a heart throb!) and of course the most common man du joir, David Cassidy!

My dad was still in the oilfield business and was gone from home, days at a time: sometimes as many as four to five days, several times in a month. Looking back, I can not even imagine how hard this must have been on my mother, not to mention daddy. I remember one time, daddy had been gone for several days and mama was anticipating his arrival home one evening around 6:00 p.m. She cooked dinner and we waited for daddy to arrive. A little after six, he called. He would be late. Mama and I ate in silence. I know she was heart broken and I wanted to make it better. I told her a few jokes that I had read in my joke book. She laughed and gave me a forced smile. I did not want her to hurt. I really felt responsible to keep her happy. Moreover, I felt like I owed it to her. I am not sure if this was a conscious feeling or thought but looking back, I really believe that I didn't want her to hurt for two reasons: 1. she had been so kind to me and 2. Without her, what would happen to me?

She put me to bed and told me to say my prayers and say a little prayer for daddy's safe return. A few minutes later, I got up out of bed and snuck down the hall to see how she was doing. I found her sitting on the back porch, crying. I hide in the hallway hoping and praying it would be alright very soon. Shortly, I saw the headlights of daddy's car pull into the drive way. He was home. I was relieved. I trotted back off to bed to finally go to sleep. Daddy was home now and he would help take care of mama.

Mama was so much fun for me and my friends. She would play basketball with us, play games with us and always play along with any scenario we were playing. She was often the grocery clerk, the babysitter or beauty shop owner.

My friend since childhood, Sandy Lambert Page, tells me her memories of my mama and spending time at our house. Sandy and I first met in Mary Kathryn Shelton's Kindergarten class. Mrs. Shelton's daughter, Jarae was also in our close circle of friends. Sandy and I have remained close over the past forty years and

whenever we are together, regardless of how much time has passed, we just pick right back up where we left off.

Mrs. Shelton, Jarae's mother, also became my piano teacher. I

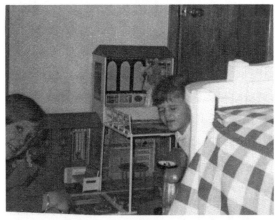

Sandy & Ronna playing with their Barbies

love the piano. I play a little by ear and despite eleven years of lessons, often my "ear" takes over and creates what it wants rather than always reading the music note for note. Looking back, I know that piano lessons must have been expensive...the lesson, the music, but there

was never any
thought that I
could and would
not take lessons.
I remember the
day that mama
picked me up
from school and
told me we had
a surprise at
home. I was in
the second

Mama Having Fun

grade. I guessed "Is it a piano?" The answer was yes. I
was so happy I cried all the drive home. I started
lessons the next week. Piano has been a wonderful
mode of expression for me over the years. Mama
would pick me up from school, take me to the lesson
and wait for me until I was done. A few years, I
remember having my lesson at noon. As soon as the
lunch bell rang, Mama would be waiting at the school
with a hot plate of lunch waiting. She always had a wet
wash cloth in a baggie for me to wash my hands before
I went in to tickle the ivories. I took lessons until I was
in the tenth grade. When I was about 11, I also took
voice lessons. I would play and sing at church, making
my parents so very proud.

I had completed grades first through fourth at South
Ward Elementary, one of three elementary schools in
Bowie. But in fifth grade, all the schools combined.
This brought new friends and new territory. I had been

a big fish in a small pond at South Ward. My best
friends and I would entertain the class every Friday
morning with songs we wrote. Jarae, Sandy, Diane, and
I would sing and play the piano.

Fifth grade tore me away from many of my familiar
friends. Those were the friends who knew where I
lived, had stayed at my house overnight, and had known
my mother and father from school parties and PTA.
Even though I was quick to make friends and I
recognized some faces from my kindergarten class six
years prior, I also remember lots of new faces. Children
have a tendency to tease and sometimes even bully other
children. But when you are on the receiving end of
teasing it is not always fun. One day from the fifth grade
sticks out in my mind to this day.

Saturday Night at Grandpa's

Sandy, Jarae, and I had been on the playground when a few of the boys and girls started teasing me about being adopted. I don't remember the cruel words that were spoken but I do remember the moments afterwards. Now, I was not the only adoptee in my class but I was the target that day. The playtime was over and we filed back into Mrs. Moore's art class. I was crying softly. Sandy, who was often my protector, walked up to Mrs. Moore's desk and told her I was sad because the children were making fun of me because I was adopted. Mrs. Moore stood and gave a speech I would never forget.

It went something like this:

"Ronna is adopted and that means that her mother and father wanted a child so bad that they waited and waited until someone gave them a baby of their own. Your parents love you too but to be adopted is a very special thing and it means you are very special and you are a wanted child."

I can remember lifting my head from my desk and thinking, "WOW, I am special." As a child, I often brought up the fact that I was adopted pretty quickly in the conversation. "Hello, I'm Ronna and I'm adopted." I was not ashamed of the fact that I was a chosen child. I am not ashamed of being adopted even today.

Growing Up Knowing

Who am I? How did I get here? Small, simple questions with such complicated answers.

There are a lot of questions and often few answers in the life of an adopted child. Sometimes we are the ones doing the asking. Sometimes it is the others doing the asking.

The most common question an adopted child gets is, "When did you find out you were adopted?" People are curious about that. I wonder why the point of discovery is such an interesting topic?

Every adopted child has a unique story about the adoption process and the discovery of this life. My story, my answer to that common question I've been asked countless times, is a simple one: I've always known that I was adopted.

I have no recollection of a specific incident, time or place when my parents told me I was adopted. I've just always known. My mother says she began telling me before I was able to understand. She would tell a beautiful, colorful story of two people, a man and a woman, who loved each other very much and wanted to share their love with someone else…and they drove to Fort Worth in the snow…and the butterfly…and the beautiful baby…and the joy. She was quite the storyteller.

She says I wanted to hear the story over and over again. I would crawl up in her lap and ask her to tell me story about when they "got" me. I don't know if I was so interested in hearing the story for understanding, comfort, or just because it was a "neat" story with a happy ending.

I know both personally and professionally that children, as part of their development, are drawn to familiar stories. Tell it again, read it again, watch it again. My godson, for example, could watch *The Lion King* all day, every day when he was young.

In treating clients who have experienced trauma, we counselors encourage them to tell the story of the traumatic event over and over. This allows clients to process the tragedy and confirm that they did survive and that they will be here tomorrow.

In 1989, I was living in an apartment that burned. Even though the apartment above me was destroyed, I did not lose any items in the fire thanks to the quick-reacting fire department. However, I was home and I noticed the smoke. I called 911 and I was panicked. Hours, even days afterwards, I told the fire story over and over again. I could not believe that it had happened to me, that I experienced the event. And even though my life was never in any real danger, it was a somewhat life-threatening experience.

I had been very, very afraid. But with each retelling of the story, the experience had less of a hold over me. My fear also had less of a hold on me. Every time I told the story, I was reminded that it was over and that I had survived.

Telling the story is a healing experience. Could it be that *hearing* the story over and over again can be just as healing?

Maybe upon hearing the story, time and time again, adopted children confirm that they are loved, that they are wanted. They confirm that they are safe and secure, even though their biological parents or birthparents have rejected them.

I can also recall when I was about 10 years old my family flew to Minnesota to visit my Grandmother Quimby who was very ill. It was my first time on an aircraft. I also remember that I was keenly aware of the flight attendants on the plane.

During the flight, I was sitting in the aisle seat and I remember looking back down the aisle. One of the flight attendants was sitting a couple of rows behind and across from me. She was reading a book. I guess she could tell she was being "watched". She looked up from her book and smiled. Did she look like me? Could this be the one who gave me up for adoption? I think I almost played "peak-a-boo" with her for a while and then my attention turned back to something else and I don't remember any further memories on the situation.

One thing about being adopted is when someone tells you that you look like someone else they know, your first thought is "could it be?" What are the chances that it could happen? You read about those stories so it does happen. Families reunited by the oddest circumstances. That is what daytime TV talk shows are made of: close encounters, family members living next door to each other and never knowing it.

Chapter 3
Belonging . . . or Not

Some people may argue that adoption is not rejection. They believe that it is receiving love or even acceptance. There was a time in my life where I would have agreed that it was 100 percent acceptance. Today, I'm not totally convinced one way or the other. The fact that it could be both, rejection and acceptance is what clouds the issues. Because that is so unclear, adoption presents an element of the "unknown." Yet another question with no simple answer.

It is all in the way that you look at it. And we may not look at it the same way every time. Many adoptees struggle with issues of abandonment or rejection. Those involved in the life of an adopted child must understand that this thread of clouded uncertainty exists in the tapestry of their life. Sometimes what an adopted child *feels* and what he or she *thinks* conflict with each other, raising all kinds of questions.

When people would question the actions of my birthmother, "Why did she give you up?" or say "I could never give up a child," I was the first one to jump to her defense. I would go into a long dissertation about how brave she was and how lucky I was that she made the decision to place me up for adoption. She was so unselfish, so sacrificing. I placed her so high on a

pedestal. I wanted to accept this as fact. By making
her the giving soul, it helped protect me from any
thoughts that I was rejected or unwanted.

However, what goes up must come down. There was
a time when my birthmother's pedestal came falling
down. The crash came with many feelings. I even
describe the feelings as anger. So in viewing this from
the other angle, the truth is...I was rejected. She was
very selfish, thinking of only herself. How could she?
But I was not a planned pregnancy. And the truth of the
matter is that if I had been conceived a few years later,
after Roe vs. Wade, I may have never been carried to
term.

Today, people are so quick to ask why women don't
"just get an abortion for an unwanted pregnancy?"
There are even situations, where I might even agree, but
knowing that **I**, being an unwanted pregnancy, could
have been aborted, does shed a different light on the
question.

On the 22nd day of January 1963, my birth was not a
celebrated occasion. This is the case for many children
who are being placed for adoption. No one came to the
hospital nursery to visit the baby. No grandparents
"oohed and awed" over the new arrival. No proud
father passed out cigars. No excitement, only a woman
who was ready to get back to her life and put this day
behind her. Thinking about all of this, it is easy to take
the view that adoption is rejection.

And with that I am sad; I had no celebration during
my first hours of life. No one to hold, comfort, and

bond with me. I started out my new life alone.

However, a few days later there was a celebration in a small trailer located on a small lot in the town of Bowie, Texas. That is the "acceptance" part. Couples sacrifice to bring an infant into their home, to offer this new life love and the many opportunities that can become available. They accept and raise the child as a member of the family. They want to start being involved with the child as early as possible.

Over the last decade, more adoptive parents have been part of their child's birth. Often the birth mother selects her unborn child's parents from a list of prospective parents, or perhaps the birthmother has answered an ad placed by an infertile couple seeking a child. In these cases, often the adoptive parents are even in the delivery room. The birth is a celebrated occasion for the new parents and their family. However, that was not the typical case in earlier years. During research for the book, I discovered that the wives of a Fort Worth doctors group would come to the nursery at the hospital and hold the babies being placed for adoption. This information brought me comfort.

So can we choose which it is, acceptance or rejection? In talking with others who are adopted, it often doesn't take long for the conversation to come to details around trying to figure out this question. "I *know* that she didn't reject me but sometimes it feels like it. What is wrong with me?" Of course, the answer to the last question is "nothing, absolutely nothing is wrong with me." But to be loved and accepted into a family, with whom you are not blood related is the ultimate acceptance. So back to the question, "Is adoption rejection in one world or is adoption the ultimate acceptance by another?" The answer is all in the way you approach the question. Sometimes the answer may depend on your mood. Maybe the answer depends on the tides, the sign of the moon, which side of the bed you awake from. I have concluded that the answer to this question for me is...maybe a little of both. It is both.

Am I happy today that I am an adopted child? Of course I am. How would I know any difference? This is my life. Although I am still in search of self and in search of more answers, I have found a peace and an understanding. The road of my life has had many turns to bring me to the place where I am today. My road today still brings new adventure and surprises that I have never dreamed. I challenge those touched by adoption to think past the borders. For this road is long and often steep. And sometimes you can lose your way.

Chapter 4
Letters in the Dark

In 1992, I was very depressed. I was suffering the pain of a broken relationship. And although we had not been dating for very long, it wasn't the first time I lost at love. Guilt, embarrassment, and shame compounded my pain. What was wrong with me that I could not succeed in the game of love?

I was in graduate school, working on my masters in counseling and just months away from graduation. Since I was a counselor in training, I did not think it was appropriate for me to admit I might need counseling. I had undergone the mandatory six sessions that the counseling program required for graduation and enjoyed each session. I agreed that all counselors should experience the position of being a client. I also believed that to be a great counselor you must be aware of your own issues. Knowing your self—"self-actualization"—is the key to helping others. But I did not want to admit my failures and feel even more vulnerable.

I was so clouded by my pain and physically ill from my depression that I didn't have the emotional strength to reach out or realize that I needed direction.

A friend from graduate school called me that one summer day. I remember barely being able to answer the telephone. I can remember the effort it took to pull

myself off the couch and go to the telephone. I told
Kathy that I felt like my skin was falling off and I was
hollow on the inside. I wasn't sleeping or eating. She
quickly gave me the number for a counselor who was a
close friend of hers. I made an appointment to see
Sheri the next day.

I had lost a lot of weight and was unable to eat. I
was truly depressed.

I don't recall exactly how the counseling sessions
progressed. But I do recall that my counselor, Sheri
Montou, was curious about my adoption, my
childhood, and issues around my failed relationship. I
remember she began immediately to draw some
conclusions connecting many of my issues to my
adoption. I was somewhat puzzled. Everything that she
was saying seemed to fit, but I did not understand how
it could all be related. I thought it was about losing
someone who I thought was the man of my dreams.

Sheri suggested that I begin doing some writings, not
only in a journal but also letters to those who were
involved in the deep feelings I was struggling with. She
asked that I write the letters in my non-dominant hand,
my left one. She would later explain that the purpose of
using the non-dominant hand is to keep your thoughts
coming at a slower rate so you can express them with
the deepest honesty and without doing a lot of
censoring as you write. I was willing to give it a try.

I started with a letter to a person who was a total
stranger — my birth mother. As I began to search my
heart, I started to feel the void of not having a

relationship with her. But on the other hand, it was difficult to admit that she was a real person, somewhere out there.

I vividly remember writing the first letter. I was house-sitting at a large ranch outside of Arlington, Texas. I went outside to escape the confines of four walls. Sitting on the patio under the blue sky, I stared at the blank sheet of paper. I looked at the pencil, just a simple writing instrument that was being asked to express some of my deepest thoughts. I did not know where to begin. It was a huge task. The wide-open space of the ranch seemed appropriate in relation to the wide-open space in my heart. I felt so small, I felt so alone. My first letter was dated 6/10/92.

Dear Mom:

I don't have or know what to say. You have always been so abstract, like a vast god or mystical power, something you just have faith in that it exists. Yet writing makes you real, flesh & blood....still...

I am 29 years old—many mistakes but you probably understand. I was a mistake but you righted the wrong by giving me to a couple who wanted me very much.

It's so unreal to try and comprehend this--I grew inside you, a part of you but my eyes know not what you look like, my ears know not what you sound like and my arms know not what you feel like.

I know it took strength to let me go but what about love . . . bittersweet.

What do I want right now? Just to know you've missed me would be, I don't know what it would be, maybe just nice to hear

I didn't sign the letter. When I read it today, although I feel that I have progressed past that initial letter, it feels so fresh. Almost ten years later, I still experience a feeling of wonder. Reaching out into a dark, vast space and not knowing if anyone is there to hear. The echo of that voice ringing and ringing. Hello...hello...hello....

Then Sheri went even further. She asked me to write a letter to my birthfather. "My who?" I thought.

Even though the letters carry the same date, I do not remember the act of writing the letter to my birthfather. But I do recall the emotions were very intense.

6/10/92

Hello,

I thought my letter to "her" was hard, but this is extremely difficult. In all honesty, I don't think about you much at all--mostly when I give your description, I think you were cute. I've got your green eyes and dark skin. I like that.

Did you love her?

I did not personalize this letter. No "Dear Dad," just a hello. Even "Hello" seemed awkward. I was reaching out to someone who rarely entered my mind. What could I say? I didn't sign it. A stranger who was so far removed, I didn't know how to make a move. And if I could, what direction should I go?

But confusion was only a small part of what I was experiencing. I was angry. I was <u>very</u> angry. All of a sudden when I read the letters over again, I was flooded with intense emotion. I was furious at both of them for very different reasons. *How could she do that? Who did he think he was? Why didn't they want me? What was wrong with me?*

That night, I had a dream about a crying infant. The mother was there holding a crying baby. She laid the small infant down in a crib and walked off, not looking back. The baby continued to cry, longing for its mother to return. Soon, another woman came in and picked the crying baby up. This woman comforted the crying infant. The baby stopped crying as the woman held the baby to her shoulder. But even though the baby was feeling safe and secure, the baby was looking at the door where the mother had exited. Through the baby's tears, the eyes were filled with longing. When I awoke, I realized, I was dreaming about myself. I was this baby.

All of a sudden I felt empty. I had honestly never experienced that part of the adoption experience: the part of being alone, the sense of rejection. I felt like a child lost at a circus with people all around, but no friendly face. A small person in a large, impersonal world. It was an experience fraught with questions, with feelings of fear, of anxiety, of sadness, and of isolation. *How could she? What was he thinking? Why?*

That was the first time **I** asked why. Others had often asked me why. And I had answered that question "why" about the whole adoption experience numerous times. Calmly and rationally, I would answer in my birthmother's defense: *She was unmarried and it was too difficult to raise a child as a single mother. What a selfless act to give up a baby so the baby can have a better life.* And even though my logic knew she had made the decision that was in the best interest of the child, my heart didn't believe it. I also asked "why?" The answer that I had given so many times to satisfy the questions of others was not enough to satisfy me. I wanted to know more. So what if she was single, so what if she was young? Why didn't she want <u>me</u>? Maybe it was the decision that was in <u>her</u> best interest but not mine! What was wrong with me? I was a real person, not an animal that could be given away to another home. Or should I say sold!

Even though I had always known I was adopted, I remember one day looking through the drawer of my Mom's cedar chest. In it, I found letters and other documents from my adoption and the maternity home. I was even more curious at this point. I sat on the floor looking at all of them and it almost felt like unveiling a secret. I didn't want to get caught reading the material. Why? It was not really a secret. But somehow, I felt like if I was discovered looking through these documents, I might hurt my parents. Would they know I was curious? Was it okay to be curious?

Twenty years later, I asked my mother to send me whatever information she had saved from the adoption process. She sent me a large envelope with several letters, brochures, and cancelled checks. There were the letters dated from 1960 (three years before my birth) and letters from shortly after my birth. There were checks made out to the agency's attorney and to the agency. Along with the checks was an itemized bill:

Reimbursement to Home for upkeep of mother . . $220.00
Harris Hospital for care of mother and child . . . $327.10
Obstetrician $120.00
Pediatrician $15.00
Court Costs (not attorney fees) $100.00
Misc: . .Layette (20.00) Medicine (50.00) Flowers (5.00)
Ambulance (10.00) Transportation (5.00) 90.00
TOTAL $872.10

It is strange looking at a statement, invoice, or receipt that documents a transaction for a baby. I don't know if looking at a hospital bill from an "ordinary" hospital maternity bill elicits similar emotions. It seems like it would be more akin to a bill from a spa for a service with a wonderful take-home bonus instead of a "bill of sale"—like when you purchase an automobile and you review all the list of items—*undercoating, loan insurance,* all the small expenses. I don't know how to share this experience, my thoughts, but I can tell you it is an unusual feeling. Searching for the phrase to describe what I have above labeled an "ordinary"

HOMESTEAD CHILD PLACEMENT
AGENCY

Date: **1-28-63**

This is to acknowledge that we have received on this day Baby

Girl Lamb   from HOMESTEAD CHILD PLACEMENT AGENCY for a period

of six (6) months, at which time we agree to formally adopt the

child as our own, or to return the child to HOMESTEAD CHILD PLACE-

MENT AGENCY in case we decide not to adopt the child. We further

agree that we will keep and maintain the child as our own and will

in no way abuse or use the child in any way other than we would

a child of our own. We have agreed to reimburse HOMESTEAD CHILD

PLACEMENT AGENCY for certain expenses which were incurred by said

Agency in connection with the upkeep of the mother of said child,

the birth of said child and legal expenses.

The following expenses were incurred:

Reimbursement to Home for upkeep of mother------------------$220.00

Harris Hospital for care of mother and child---------------- 327.10

Dr. Jack Turner, Obstretrician----------------------------- 120.00

Dr. Harry Womack, Pediatrician----------------------------- 15.00

Dependency proceedings and Court costs---------------------- 100.00

Layette---------$ 20.00 Transportation--------$5.00
Medicine-------- 50.00
Flowers--------- 5.00
Ambulance------- 10.00
                                           $90.00

TOTAL---------------------------$ ~~90.00~~
                                 $ 872.10

HUSBAND'S FULL NAME_____

hospital stay was such a difficult task. I wanted to compare the experience of my birth to a birth of a child who would be taken home by the same woman who gave birth to her. But I can't seem to find the words or phrases.

But again, this pregnant woman did give birth. Then she left to get her life back to "normal." Who knew if she would ever look back?

Then there was "him." Who was he? The questions surrounding my birthfather did not center on "why?" but more about who he was and the circumstances of his role in all this. Did he hold the key to my troubled personal relationships with men? I did not want to acknowledge that he existed, but since he did exist, I decided to acknowledge him and then I decided that I hated him.

As the months went by, I continued to write more letters to the two individuals who I had never met.

To my birthmother:

10/27/93

To my mother--All my questions remain unanswered--answers I may never find. The opening of one door leads only to another one that is closed. Who holds the key? Everyday I feel the pain, emptiness, like an empty well echoing my pleas for understanding. I cannot walk away from the emptiness because it beckons my heart-leaving me only to face it and heal.

Heal? How can I heal without the answers to which I seek? I have yet to see your smiles, hear your voice and feel your touch....over thirty years. But this heart that you gave life to beats strong. My mind is full of wisdom and my soul is full of courage. So my heart will survive the pain in feeling our loss--my mind will learn to understand and my soul will guide the journey.

Who am I? I am pretty. I am loving, kind, and gentle. I am your daughter. I am all I am. I am enough.

To my birthfather:

10/27/93

Hello-

What do I call you? I am still very angry with you. I have always held to the question if SHE thought of me? She endured the nine months and pain of labor. Did you want to be there? Did you know of my birth? Do you remember the date? Did you know I'm a girl and <u>you</u> are my daddy—wow— you are my daddy. Can I call you daddy? Daddy. Daddy. Daddy--even looks misspelled. Daddy, daddy—I'm your little girl. And I smile real nice.

I was beginning to make peace. I no longer hated him. I no longer doubted her choice. Maybe the healing was beginning. The process was evolving that there was nothing wrong with me. I was not mad at my birthmother, birthfather, adoptive-mother, adoptive father, or myself.

A Question of Semantics

"Birthparent" is a word that has become part of my vocabulary. It is not a term that all individuals use on a regular basis. Those children born to the parents who are raising them do not need the word "birthparent" in their vocabularies. They don't refer to their parents as my "birthmom" and birthfather".

As I started my search, I have used the term "birth family" over and over again. When I sit here and think about the term, it feels strange. Maybe it is because the term is one that I use to describe a stranger. Someone with whom I have a deep genetic bond, but that is a stranger to my eyes, my touch, and my ears. *"Birthmother"* to me is a person, someone real, not just a term to describe the biological connection.

Another interesting issue regarding birthparents is the overuse of the term "birthmother" and rare use of the term "birthfather." There are hundreds of birthmothers searching for their children, but rarely do I see a birthfather. Most people ask if I know who my "mother" is. Rarely does one ask about my birthfather. I'm somewhat puzzled by that. It takes two people, a man and a woman, to create a baby, so why ask about one and not the other?

Recently, in talking at lunch with a group of friends, I noted that I rarely hear about birthfathers. Hours later, one of the men in the group asked if he could speak to me privately. He told me that twenty years ago he had gotten a girl pregnant and they placed the child, a boy, up for adoption. He went on to tell me that he had never told anyone. Only his mother knew, even though he was now married with daughters. He was very close to his wife and daughters, but he said that he constantly thought about "his son" who was somewhere out there.

He said he would be open to a reunion if the child sought him out, but he did not know where to turn to find the now 19-year-old male child. Did the child even want to know?

Granted, I am guilty of focusing on my birthmom. For years I would talk of her often, but the only time I would speak of "him" is when I would rattle off the description of his physical characteristics. My birthmom has blond hair, and blue eyes and I have dark eyes, dark skin, and dark hair, like him.

Texas laws did not require that when a child is placed for adoption that both biological parents must give their permission. This is something I just discovered. I have to trust that the man described as my father is <u>actually</u> my father.

Is the description that was given to my mother on the day the adoption agency called real? Was she a blonde? Was she a flight attendant? Did she give the correct information? Did he know I was on the way? Did his family know? The questions seemed endless and I had very few answers.

Chapter 5
Unlucky in Love

Unlucky in love, always losing the game,
I'd try again but they all end the same.
Just me, alone, in the dark.

That is the opening sentence from a song I wrote many years ago.

What is the connection between adoption and losing the game of love? Or is there a connection? Have we already lost a significant relationship in our life? Are we now searching, looking to fill the voids in our life? Often, we may go from relationship to relationship in search of a love that will not leave us, alone in the dark. Finding this love would prove to ourselves that we are worthy, we are lovable, we are OK, and people won't leave.

We enter into relationships and then begin to wait for the other shoe to drop. This person will leave me, too. Just wait and see. We may even set up the relationship to fail. Then when our partner does leave (because we ultimately have designed it so they will) we validate our feelings of inadequacy. "See, I knew no one would love me forever!" "No one wants me forever." "There is something wrong with me, because people leave me, I'm unlovable." There is not a conscious connection to the fact that we are adopted, but the issue lies deep within until we have the courage to understand it.

What dynamics must be present or absent for this to occur? Granted, there are many people who are not adopted and experience relationship troubles. In working with clients who report such self-destructive, relationship-sabotaging behavior, nine times out of ten the client has some experience with abandonment.

Alone in the Dark

Abandonment issues consume many lives. Abandonment. Feeling alone. Many of us have experienced an actual abandoning of a parent. Maybe the parent is still living under the same roof, but, due to depression, addiction or other issues, we perceive the parent has "left" us because he or she is are not available emotionally. Some parents even physically abandon their children. But with all physical abandonment comes emotional abandonment, and with emotional abandonment, physical abandonment also is experienced to some degree.

Fear of abandonment is very real to the people involved. Those who have been abandoned usually blame themselves as the cause of the parent's leaving or unavailability.

The question is this: Is placing a child up for adoption the equivalent of abandonment?

Webster's New American Dictionary defines "abandon" as *to leave or forsake completely and finally*

. . . To leave or forsake completely and finally. Those words cut deep.

In 1999, in Oregon the voters passed Measure 58, which would allow adult adoptees to see sealed birth certificates. One of the opponents, a birth mother, was quoted as saying, "The idea of the adoption was to permanently sever the relationship with the child." (Fort Worth Star-Telegram 8/28/99) *Permanently sever* sounds like a "final" statement to me.

Whatever the cause of the "abandonment," the void it leaves is real and as a result, the search is on to fill the void. The search is on to find the answers. When we are abandoned, we are left vulnerable. When we are vulnerable, we feel like a child. All of these feelings are usually the driving force in our search for relationships as well as the underlying force in the destruction of the relationships.

Speaking from my own trouble in relationships, I can now recognize that I was searching for something. And when I would find what could be a possible loving relationship, I would keep the protective walls of my heart intact, so I would not get hurt. Looking back, I would not allow myself to fall in love for fear that I would be left, crying, alone in the dark.

Even after finding love, I often find myself ready to jump into the pool of insecurities and tell myself that no one really loves me, no one really wants me. It is a constant battle. The self-doubt is sometimes almost unbearable.

Through exploring issues of relationships, I discovered a part of myself that was a little disturbing. I would abandon relationships believing that the people I left would feel no pain or sadness. They would not care. It would not make an impact on them. I had not realized that my actions did affect other people. The reasoning (illogical as it might be) was the fact that because I was the one to leave and that no one *really* cared, then no one would really care if I was there at all. I was off the hook.

I can remember after breaking up with a boyfriend, he told me how sad he was. I was shocked. He was actually sad. I couldn't even comprehend that I had meant that much to him. He had told me he loved me, but somehow that didn't matter. I was not in love with him so I was blind to his love for me.

After trying to look at this pattern in my life, I came to the conclusion that somewhere in my heart I didn't feel like I really matter. I felt insignificant. It was like that baby looking over the shoulder of the woman who was trying to comfort her but because of the longing for the mother that had walked out the door, the baby felt insignificant and almost invisible.

I shared this discovery with a friend who was also adopted. She sat there in silence and said, "You know, I do that too." Could this behavior of relationship abandonment be a result from growing up an adopted child, a child who was given away at birth?

It took me some time to realize that I was lovable. I actually mattered to others and then even to myself.

Part of the difficulty in making this realization was it didn't make sense to me. How could I feel insignificant when I had been so engulfed in love from my adoptive parents?

I was a well behaved child. I didn't get into any significant trouble. I didn't run with the "wrong crowd" or experiment with drugs or cigarettes. Looking back, part of my being well behaved was out of a sense of loyalty to my parents. They had in fact "taken me in" when no one else wanted me. How could I do anything that would hurt them or disappoint them?

During the time I had to write the letters to my birthparents, I remember being mad at my mom and dad. It was short lived but I think it was valid emotion. My thought was "how could you buy me like a piece of property?"

Just sitting there letting the emotions flow, I remember the experience. As the tears trailed down my face, I felt more whole. The rain of my tears was washing my pain and insecurities away. I felt "visible." I mattered. I mattered to my parents. I mattered to my family. I mattered to my friends and for the first time I mattered to me.

This evolution was what I needed to take the next step in my journey.

Chapter 6
The Search

"Have you ever thought about trying to find your birthmother?" "Do you know who your mother is?" These are other questions that people frequently ask. Ironically, I had just begun working on this topic of searching and was talking with a friend about the fact I was writing a book about my adoption experience. Her first words where the exact, verbatim question that is at the top of this page. *"Have you ever thought about trying to find your birthmother?"*

Have I ever thought about it? Of course, I have. I still think about it. How could you not at least think about the possibility of meeting the person who gave birth to you? People have many opinions regarding this issue. I have heard from non-adopted people that they would <u>have</u> to know, or some say they would <u>never</u> need to know. For those who say that they have no need to know, I am certain that they have at least wondered.

I have never had the burning desire to begin a search. My life has been very fulfilling. The void has not caused any major damage. I often think of my birthmom on my birthday. I have thought of her for at least the last 30 years. Does she remember this date? Does she remember the moment? Does she think and wonder about me?

After collecting my thoughts for this book, I thought maybe a search would be…shall I say "interesting". So in 1999, I registered with the Texas state adoption register. It was a simple registration. I just sent in some basic information and if the biological parents or other family member had registered the match would occur. I really was unsure if I even wanted to know. I did not have any expectations. I was not going to give it a second thought. It was just a basic first step, just in case.

Unexpectedly, I soon received a letter from the Texas Department of Human Services, Adoption Registry. "Oh my god." My heart began to beat out of my chest. I reread the return address and tried to think of what else it could have been. I never expected to hear anything. What was this all about? I carefully opened the letter and read the first line.

"Thank you for your registration, unfortunately, no match was made."

No matches were made? Disappointment set in. But why was I disappointed? I wasn't really searching. I just sent it in because I was writing a book and thought maybe this was an unspoken requirement. But my feeling was true disappointment. I was sad. Maybe, I did want to know. I was searching. Maybe I did not know exactly what I was searching for but I was definitely feeling disappointed, so I must have been wanting something. I have been telling myself for years, that I would like to search to get the medical records. Any medical information would be helpful. It would provide answers to many questions that so many take for granted. It is amazing how many times we are asked about our family history of health and I never knew any of those answers. That is another "disability" that adoptees experience: no medical history. Does heart disease run in my family? Did the women in my family fight the battle of breast cancer? What is waiting for me, health wise, down the road?

But . . . those answers were not to be found today, for the letter read "no match".

Just as well, I told myself. I have always been afraid to search, sort of like opening Pandora's box. What would happen? Would the reunion be joyful or painful? What secrets would be discovered? After getting the information, there would be no covering it up again.

I am by nature a very curious person. I thought if I could just find the address to my birthmother's home, I could to sit in my car across the street and observe her life. See what she looked like; get a sense of her style without having to get involved in all the emotionality of it. Just sit and watch. Sounds a bit like stalking.

But would that be enough, or would I then want to take the next step and stir up a conversation with her? Maybe pass myself off as an Avon lady and just look in her eyes and listen to her voice. I'm a professional counselor; I could shift the conversation and get her to tell me a little bit about her life.

But inevitably the next step would be too hard to resist. I wouldn't be able to stop, just there. I would stutter and hem-ha around with my heart pounding and then say "Hello, my name is Ronna. I was born on January 22, 1963, in Fort Worth, Texas. Remember what you were doing on that day? Surprise, it's a girl!"

What would her reaction be? Would I find a door being slammed in my face? Would I be embraced? Would I be denied? Would I discover a group of people that I share a gene pool and be totally overwhelmed? Would the skeletons in this family closet be something that I could not escape? That is what makes this so frightening.

When I read an article about the Oregon cases on one Saturday afternoon, I felt an empty pit in the bottom of my stomach. The birthmother stated that she did not want to be "hunted down".

Would she feel like game being hunted down? Would she welcome me or tell me to get the hell out? The fear and pain of being rejected again would be more than I could bear. I'd rather not risk it, at least not yet.

That is why the registry is such a good idea. That confirms that both parties desire to meet the other. But according to *my* registration, she has no desire to meet me or was unaware that the registry exists. But it felt more like the first scenario—no desire to meet me. I figured I'd just have to wait.

I decided to take another step into the world of searching. I registered with numerous on-line registries. How they work is that you post your information and it is placed on a web page and furthermore, everyone who is on this registry gets an email of your post. So in case someone posts some information, I get the email. For several years, I received numerous emails of new entries on the registry. All in the same format:

Child name

Date of birth

Birth mother name

I checked out the ones that are from the state of Texas and quickly deleted when I saw that the date of birth, city, and county do not match. I wondered what the scene would be if I ever saw my personal information on the screen

Child name: unknown baby girl

Date of Birth: January 22, 1963, Fort Worth, Texas

Mother's Name: Jane Doe

. . . and we have a match. But every day, I deleted e-mail after e-mail of entries that did not match. She was not there. My conclusion was that she was not looking, that she was not interested. I just did not know. Then maybe again, maybe email was just not her thing.

Adopted children just don't know.

Homestead — A visit to the location

As mentioned earlier, my birthmother went to Homestead Maternity Home in Fort Worth, Texas. My parents had old brochures and would talk openly about the agency if I asked.

I discovered the name of a couple who were once "foster parents" for Homestead. I had not known that they used foster parents. The name of the couple was in a local newspaper article dated 1999 regarding a

"Homestead Reunion" that was held in Fort Worth: Mr. and Mrs. Stone. Through contacting the Stones, I was put in touch with birthmothers and other adoptees from Homestead. My first connection.

Back in 1992, I had tracked down the address of the Maternity Home on Rosedale Drive in Fort Worth. I drove up and down the street countless times looking for the address. Where was it? Finally, I discovered that the address I was searching for was now a parking lot. The houses across the street bore a very similar look to the picture of the home listed on the Homestead brochure. I parked my car, stepped out, and looked around. My heart was pounding. *She* had been here before. *She* had looked at those very same houses, the very same trees, the very same view of the hospital district. This first connection to my birthmother—a parking lot on land where she once lived—was so overwhelming. I found myself crying in my car. I was soon in contact through email to birthmothers who had given birth to their children around the time I was being born. Could some of these women remember my birthmother? I would anxiously await the next reunion to meet some of them and hear about Homestead Maternity Home….my beginning.

The Homestead Reunion

I did not know what to expect when I attended the reunion that rainy Saturday in May. I was very anxious about going. The dark skies mirrored of how I was feeling. I soon was to discover that maybe every thing that I had been told was not the whole truth.

First, the location I had sought out from the brochure was the location that the home moved to in February 1963. I was born in January 1963, so it is doubtful that my birthmother stayed at that location. Sounds silly, but I felt almost a sense of loss. We had not shared the same view of the hospitals, the trees or the houses. We were once again "apart".

As I sat in the corner of the room, I also discovered that most of the adoptees were told that their birthparents were "flight attendants and doctors", with "highly marketable" characteristics". My parents had not been told the "doctor" part but the rest seem to fit and I was fearful that maybe the woman in my mind who was my birthmother was not an accurate picture. All these years in my mind she was a flight attendant and maybe that was just a persona so my adoptive parents would believe she was a attractive person.

There were many birthmothers and adoptees there that had been reunited. I was curious how this happened, since the lid was closed so tightly on the adoption records. They even talked about how when Homestead closed, the records were taken out to a field and burned. It is reported that upon the closing of the facility, the director and another board member took all the records out to a ranch and burned them. It is said that they were concerned that they would get in the wrong hands. Years later in 1984 the Texas legislature required closing agencies to turn the records over to the state. According to the Texas Department of State

Health Services Closed Adoption-Agency records of vital statistics, it states that only an index exists of some of the children placed for adoption by Homestead Maternity. "No agency records have ever been located". Finding the woman who had given birth to me now seemed hopeless. The only information that would still exist would be the original birth certificate. I would have to have her name to get this released and possibly would need her "permission" first. Any information was possibly up in smoke or would be like finding a needle in a haystack. But a few things happened. I met two women.

The first was a birthmother who had been reunited with her son who had sought her out. He was born a week after me. She looked at me and said, "You look just like your mother". I was taken aback. She started to describe her and it did fit the description my parents had been given. She was a flight attendant. I was amazed. I was standing in front of a woman who had actually talked with my birthmother. I reached out to touch her hand. I swallowed hard. This was a special moment.

Usually, I am the life of the party. But this day, I was quiet, introspective, introverted and continued to sit in the corner. Although my eyes were very moist, I was not crying. It was to overwhelming to cry. I just sat there listening, watching everyone interact.

I learned that the assumed name that the girls were given when they entered the home started with the same letter as their actual name. The infant was usually given

the name "Baby girl…..or Baby boy….name". My
paperwork said, "Baby girl Lamb". My mom had once
mentioned the name Lockhart. I am not sure where she
had heard or read the name but she had mentioned it.
They both started with the letter "L." Lockhart. It had
to be right.

The second woman I met was Bonnie. She was an
intermediary, a searcher for adoptees. We talked about
how she reunited adoptees and birthfamilies. The first
step would be to petition the court to open my adoption
records and then let her get to work. I got her business
card and for the next 30 days, I found myself staring it.
I wondered what the road ahead of me would be and
which direction I would go and what I would find.

I had never dwelled on the idea of searching for my
birthmother. I did think of her on occasion and
remember looking at the window at the moon and
thinking that she was definitely somewhere out there.

To Court

I had stared long enough. I actually was almost void
of emotions so I sat down and I wrote a letter to the
judge of the 96th District Court to request the opening of
my records. I was soon called and was given a court
date to appear before District Judge Jeff Walker. I did
not know what to expect but I was not giving up. What
did I have to lose?

I took my friend Judith for moral support. Judith
and I met in graduate school and soon discovered that
we had a very special friendship. I called her my "safe"

friend, one that I could tell my deepest, darkest thoughts and feelings to and she would still be there for me. Since this was an event of many emotions—they were all over the place—she seemed like the most logical choice.

It could have not gone more smoothly. On the stand, I talked about Bonnie and what I wanted. I was searching for medical records first. If a relationship were to emerge between me and my birthmother, that would be welcomed as well. The judge appointed Bonnie to my case and said he would open the records to her and she could search. I was to pay $160 to the court for an escrow account for Bonnie's expenses and fees. She would request my original birth certificate from Austin. I was not to be told my birthmother's name or location.

Judith & Ronna

When Bonnie located her, she would contact her and let her know I was looking and then with her consent, we would be united. The process could take years or could take only a few months. The wait began.

Chapter 7
Her Name was . . . Betsy

Only a few weeks later I received an email from my search angel. It had only been a short time since she requested my birth certificate. An email message popped up on the screen of my laptop with the subject line "update." I was afraid to open it. With my heart pounding, I read her words:

> *Ronna, not much news, found that your birth mother is from a Northern State, no town or county shown, they gave the address of the Maternity Home, the birth father is deceased, I will let you know as soon as I have any news.*

"The birth father is deceased." I wanted to cry but at the same time was extremely numb. I would never know him. He would never know me. Was I to grieve? Had I actually lost anything? It was a strange feeling. I had just lost something I had never had.

Bonnie told me that he was born and raised and died in Hawaii. This made some sense since in the original description his occupation was listed as a recreational instructor at a hotel, teaching activities, like surfing. Not much surfing in the Gulf of Mexico.

I found out that I had been right in suspecting my birthmother's name was Lockhart. I had even been given a hint by one of the birthmothers at the reunion. Her name was "Betsy." And I knew it was short for Elizabeth, I just knew. As it turned out, I was right—my birthmother's name was Elizabeth Lockart. But even with her name it was going to be a needle in a haystack search. We had a name and a state. No city, no address, no date of birth. Bonnie needed more information. She requested the hospital records from the court. Again, we would have to play the waiting game. Time was passing at a snail's pace.

On November 28, 2001, I started my week with my search weighing on my mind. It had been months since I had heard from Bonnie. I quickly sent off a "Hey don't forget me" email to her. She replied quickly and gave her apologies for all the dead ends that we kept facing. She had even called several women, checking out each possibility but with no results. I fully understood.

I too had tried my hand at searches on the Internet. When I would type in my birthmother's name, I would get lots of matches but there was no way to narrow it down. I had learned from another birthmom that her middle name was usually considered a "last name." I wouldn't even attempt to guess. And yet, another blank. But I would put in the information I did know and hit enter. Results would come but there were countless Lockharts and even more Elizabeths.

On this day, strictly out of habit, I went to rootsweb.com and typed in her first and last name. I anticipated my daily ritual: Up would spring the page that would show me all the matches but no exact matches in the databases listed. However, I often would pick one out and click on it and scan the first 100 or so Elizabeths or Lockharts, depending on my mood du jour. I did not know what I was looking for but one never knows.

That day there was a new listing. I saw where the alumni list had one match . . . so, I clicked on it.

On the screen read the following:

Lockhart, Elizabeth Wilson   Class of 1957   New Castle HS   PA

My mouth dropped open. My heart was beating out of my chest. I pushed my chair away from my desk like it was something contaminated. I was speechless.

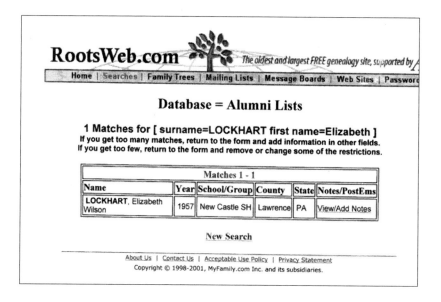

RootsWeb.com

The oldest and largest FREE genealogy site, supported by

Home | Searches | Family Trees | Mailing Lists | Message Boards | Web Sites | Password

Database = Alumni Lists

1 Matches for [surname=LOCKHART first name=Elizabeth]
If you get too many matches, return to the form and add information in other fields.
If you get too few, return to the form and remove or change some of the restrictions.

| | | | Matches 1 - 1 | | |
Name	Year	School/Group	County	State	Notes/PostEms
LOCKHART, Elizabeth Wilson	1957	New Castle SH	Lawrence	PA	View/Add Notes

New Search

About Us | Contact Us | Acceptable Use Policy | Privacy Statement
Copyright © 1998-2001, MyFamily.com Inc. and its subsidiaries.

There in black and white: Lockhart.....Elizabeth...a last name, Wilson...1957 (matched my calculations of possible graduation date) and Pennsylvania...that was the northeast!

I walked across the hall to my co-worker, Rebekah's. Calmly I said, "Rebekah? Can you please come to my office?" It was so nonchalant that it was almost robotic.

Sitting back down, my hands covered my face. My eyes grew wide in bewilderment. Could it be? How could it be? Was this it? The true needle in the haystack?

I told Rebekah what I discovered. Then my hands shaking, I then typed in a search for the high school in an alumni database. There she was again.....and this time she was listed as "Betsy." I had her email address — not the actual address — but at least an avenue to email her.

Fellow co-workers quickly discovered what I had uncovered. In trying to speak to them about the day's events, I began to cry. I wasn't crying because I was sad or even because I was happy, I was just overwhelmed. It had happened. I had located this person whom I was a part of...someone I didn't know but someone who I couldn't deny was my life-force. All those years of having information about that somewhere out "there" was now <u>here</u>.

I immediately contacted Bonnie and told her that I thought that I had actually found my birthmother. I gave Bonnie the information and she then took the lead.

Doing her magic, Bonnie soon turned the name into an address, a telephone number, and a birth date. She quickly gathered information to contact her and asked me to prepare a letter from me to include in the packet.

A letter from me . . . I had been practicing this letter for years but now that it was actually time to write it, I hit a wall. My birthmother had always been there with me tucked away in a small part of my heart, now that I was closer to meeting her than I ever was; she felt a million miles away. I was afraid. Afraid of exactly what, I did not know.

Chapter 8
First Contact

I wanted to get the letter done as quickly as possible but I was finding it very difficult to complete. I had practiced, rehearsed what I would say on my first meeting. I had actually written a couple of letters to have on hand, just in case. I looked at some of the drafts I had worked on two years ago. What does one write to encourage someone to be a part of your life, to let them know you are not a sick, crazy lunatic out to disrupt their life. But was that how this whole thing would be perceived? A major disruption? An unwanted weed springing up in a beautiful garden. I did not want to cause her any pain, but maybe it would provide some closure for her as well. That night I sat on the bed with all the drafts around me and by the time I decided to fall asleep, all I had to show for the evening was more incomplete drafts. I was void of any emotion. I was completely numb.

The next day, I started from scratch and in one attempt, wrote the letter that I had been struggling with. It would have to do...

A Warm Hello, for my birth mother:
I'm very excited to have this opportunity to write this letter. And although I've anticipated this moment

and practiced this introduction countless times, the words now seem useless. I want to share a few brief thoughts and look forward to sharing even more in the future.

I want to thank you for your strength and courage. The difficult decision you made years ago afforded me the chance to be part of a wonderful family. I was raised by two good, honest people. I am an only child and did not have the privilege of having a relationship with brothers and sisters, but I was fortunate enough to have a close-knit family.

My childhood was filled with friends, piano lessons, voice lessons, twirling, talent shows and lots of laughter.

Today, I'm a successful, independent, strong woman. I'm a licensed professional counselor (LPC) and work in management of a non-profit agency. I consider myself practical, level-headed and a darn good joke teller!

A few of my favorite things include horses, books, writing, deserts, and mountains and "I Love Lucy" reruns. Maybe you share some of my interests--I can't wait to find out.

I do not intend to be disruptive or intrusive. You will find me to be a very trustworthy, respectful, appropriate adult. I look forward to finally having a medical history!

There is so much left to say. This is only the beginning. I'd love to share my world with you. I'm enclosing the words of a very special song--one that is dear to me and speaks of our story.

I look forward to tomorrow. Until then . . .

Love-your birthdaugther, R

Somewhere out there beneath the pale moonlight, someone's thinking of me and loving me tonight.

Somewhere out there someone's saying a prayer that we'll find one another in that big somewhere out there. And even though I know how very far apart we are, it helps to think we might be wishin' on the same bright star. And when the night wind starts to sing a lonesome lullaby, it helps to think we're sleeping underneath the same big sky.

Somewhere out there if love can see us through, then we'll be together, somewhere out there, out where dreams come true.

I wrote the letter on rose-colored linen paper. I sent it to Bonnie along with a signed release of information. It would soon be on its way…an unknown destination to me but hopefully not for long. Until then, I would have to wait. I was anticipating a wait of about two weeks. That could mean a possible holiday reunion: Merry Christmas.

Christmas came and went. A week before the 25th, Bonnie had told me that the court allowed her to send a second, or follow-up letter, at three weeks. The first letter was sent on November 30, 2001. Three weeks would be smack dab in the middle of the holidays. Due to the usual hustle and bustle of the holidays, we both agreed that we would wait until after the New Year. I sure didn't want my one and only allowable follow-up to be discarded with the annual Christmas cards.

I was unable to label the feelings I was experiencing during these weeks. I felt so alone inside. Who do you talk to about this sort of thing? It is hard for others to relate to such an unusual situation. I do know that I felt sad. Not just sad because I had not heard anything but also because I may have caused her pain. I imagined that she had the whole situation tightly locked away and BAM with a delivery from the U.S. Postal Service, her world came tumbling down. The emotion, the pain, all brought to the surface again.....erupting like a volcano and covering a land which will never be the same again. Because how do you lock something like this away **again** after it had been opened? Oh, my God . . . What did I do? What have I done?" I wondered.

Regardless of what was unlocked or in limbo, on January 9, 2002, a second letter was sent. Once again, words failed me in my attempt to explain how I felt. I pride myself on being able to sit back, experience the moment and describe my inner feelings with some fantastic descriptive word. But throughout the experience, there never seemed to be the right word to describe my feelings. Numbness, sadness, overwhelmed, thrilled . . . all good words but were they accurate?

This time the second letter, written only by Bonnie, gave her the option of saying "no." Bonnie asked her to let us know either way. She informed her that I was a "normal" adult and if she could at least send medical history information we would be appreciative. Would I be in store for a reunion or a rejection? My birthday was only days away . . . maybe this "holiday" would be more of a reunion: Happy Birthday.

January 17, 2002, Bonnie called and left a message on my cell phone. She reported "I have a letter, give me a call." I could not make it back to my office fast enough. I didn't want to call her from my cell phone from the car. I was afraid of a bad connection and I wanted to be sure I heard every word and I was afraid I couldn't concentrate on my driving. Arriving back at the office, I called her immediately. She informed me that she had received a letter along with a medical history. She read the letter to me over the phone. It wasn't really a rejection, but there were no plans for any type of reunion, at least not yet.

Dear Bonnie:

Enclosed is the medical history you have requested for my birth daughter.

Needless to say after almost 40 years, this has come as a great shock to me. I do not think I can handle this right now. No one in my family ever knew about it and I don't think they could handle it either.

I am not a mean or a cruel person. I never had any other children and to know that she wants to get to know me boggles my mind. I really don't know how to act. I'm scared and really at a lost on how to handle this.

Please give me some more time on this, but I can't promise I can do it. I want her to have this medical information, as I know she needs it. I only hope she is in good health and is a happy person. I wish her nothing but love and a good and happy life.

Thank you and please give her my love and best wishes.

The name was blacked out….rules of the court. Attached were two pages of an extensive medical history. I read the letter over and over again. Bonnie pointed out how she acknowledged that I was indeed her birth daughter and Bonnie was certain that with such a kind and endearing letter that it was only a matter of time until she would be ready to embrace what I had to offer.

I reminded myself that I also had access to her through the Internet in the alumni database. I would process all this information and then decide how to proceed.

As for the medical history….her mother died when she was an infant, there was extensive history of breast cancer in the family, she had one brother. It was amazing that all of a sudden I had such important information. Information that had been asked of me many times and I had never known the answer. This was at least one step closer...more than I ever had before and more than I had expected. I did have some new feelings of "belonging." To never have answers to so many questions that other take for granted was huge. Any time you visit a new doctor, you are often asked to complete the general medical history questions.

Family history of heart disease? Diabetes? Cancer? I had always left these questions blank...but NOW....I actually had some answers and could complete the forms, just like most of the others in the waiting rooms across hospitals everywhere. That might not sound like much but this was HUGE for me. A real sense of belonging was starting to grow in my soul. I thought of finding a new doctor JUST to fill out some forms!

The original letter came to me in the mail a few days letter: A beautiful handwritten letter: mine to keep. I tucked it away for safe keeping but kept a copy in my purse to read whenever the mood hit me.

Me with Mama and Daddy in 2001.

Chapter 9
It is Time

It had been about three months since I had
received the letter from my birthmother, who I now
knew was Elizabeth Wilson Lockhart Blowers. Blowers
was the name listed through the alumni database.
Although her name had been blacked out, I knew all of
this from my lucky Internet search in the alumni
database. Through the same database I could email her.
I would frequently check the database to make sure she
was still there. Again, I wanted to contact her but not
knowing her situation made me hesitate. She had written
that no one ever knew. I didn't want her to have to do a
lot of explaining. I didn't want to rub salt in an old
wound. But one day on March 6, I concluded that it
was time. I don't recall what led me to the decision that
it was time, moreover the right time. But nevertheless, I
was determined. Through the alumni database, I
emailed her. I knew that it would come up on her
computer as "You have a message from Ronna
Quimby." She wouldn't know who the heck Ronna
Quimby was; nevertheless, I had to do it. I don't
remember any huge emotions during this time.. I wrote
only a few lines.

Suddenly, I froze . . . somehow the "send" button
looked like a huge red button that might be the one to
set off the atomic bomb..if I hit "execute" it might just

do that . . . I called out for Rebekah to come read what I had written. She "approved" and encouraged me to send it. I sat with my hand on the mouse, hovering over the send button but no clicking! Rebekah reached out, placed her hand on top of mine and guided the cursor to

Rebekah Oursler & Ronna

the unforgiving "SEND" button. The unforgiving "send" button, because once you hit it, there is no turning back. I had come so far, there was no turning back…my hand hovered over the SEND button…CLICK. The email was on its way.

I would like to get to know you and hoped that email would be a safe way. *Hope you are well. ~R*

Maybe the "R" would link her back to the letter she had received last November. Surely she remembered that letter "R" from the day that her world came crashing down….oh, crap. Fortunately she did remember.

The next morning, a Friday morning, I arrived at my office and was not thinking about the bomb I had launched the day before. Honestly not ever thinking that there might be some response. I sat at my desk and as my morning ritual, logged on to check my email.

Checking for new messages.......receiving new messages . . . And there it was! Right there in my inbox...an email reply from Betsy Blowers. This time my mouse had no trouble in finding the button to open my mail.

Her opening line said it all;

"Don't fall over but it's me!" Whoa!

The email made me laugh and cry almost at the same time. Several lines were so similar to things that I would have said:

> *Dear Ronna—don't fall over—it is me—This has been quite a shock to my system and I am slowly recovering—I don't want you to ever think that I did not want to get to know you—it is just something I never thought would happen and since I have kept this secret for soooo many years—it has taken me awhile to adjust. Really don't know where to start. I am 62 years old-married (at 43) to a great guy who is the only one that would put up with me after all these years. My family gave up on me ever getting married but I finally found the right one. I flew for Braniff and lived in Dallas for years and loved it. Came back home and worked in the travel business and have traveled all over the US and Europe. No grass under these feet. I have had one exciting life. We live in New Jersey near Atlantic City and go the shore every*

*summer. I still work but not very much—getting
lazy in my old age. You have to tell me about
you and your life too. I have pixs if you would
like to see what your ole' ma looks like—
probably will think it is your sister since I am not
old enough to have an almost 40 year old
daughter—yikes!! I hope I haven't rambled on
too much. I want to hear from you and you fill
me in on EVERYTHING. By the way, Ray and I
are considered the BEST joke tellers in Jersey
and your mom is a ham—gets up and sings with
bands—her one song "All of me" (key of F).
Was a speech and drama major in college and a
frustrated song and dance girl. So this is where
you get all your talent. I have lots more to say
but will close for now. You take care and write
when you can. So glad to hear from you. Love,
Betz*

What a joy. I read the email over and over. It was
evident that she remembered the details of MY letter—
joke teller, etc. And she was funny. Oh, this was going
to be fun.

She had a very adventuresome life and was currently
working as a blackjack dealer in Atlantic City. This was
getting more fun and exciting at every turn!!!

And thus, this began about a seven week period of a
wonderful email relationship. We kept the World Wide
Web afire. At least one email each day, maybe two or
three. We emailed stories, pictures. I sent her several
pictures of me, at various ages. Betsy emailed:

Just got home and guess what was in the mailbox —YOUR PICTURES. I am in awe, are you SURE you are my flesh and blood? . . . I am in shock-disbelief-proud-happy and every other adjective you can think of...This is a HOOT, I am so happy for us—now if I can get the courage to tell the rest of the family, we will be set.

We continued to share emails daily. Lots of great stories and photographs. She sent me a photograph of her mother, Helen. Helen had died three months after Betsy was born. When I opened the photo of Helen attached to an email I gasped. It looked like me. It really looked like ME! Weird.....looking so much like someone...FINALLY! We shared so much. Then one day we shared a phone number.

The first call was a little nerve-racking. I felt like we had developed a relationship through our countless emails but I was nervous to take the next step. I dialed. She answered. I sighed a breath of relief.

She briefly told me about my birth father, how their "relationship" had started and ended. She was apologetic for everything. Apologetic? Seemed almost weird....I didn't feel like I needed an apology, but she verbalized her sorrow several times.

She admitted she didn't remember the exact day of the month? Was it on 23rd? 21st? 22nd? All those years I was certain that at least on my birthday, she and I were making a connection but now I realized that had not been the case. Did it make any difference now? It was maybe a little disappointing but the disappointment was small compared to the excitement of what was happening.

Her apologies, I realized, were a part of her healing process just like I had come to heal. She had never told anyone in her life, except to her husband Ray.

As things got serious with Ray, she causally mentioned that she had once had a baby and given it up for adoption and then changed the subject. He never raised the subject again.

Helen Wilson Lockhart
My Maternal Grandmother

She was raised in a prominent family and couldn't bare the shame and possible disowning that she feared. So at this point she had only told her husband of our reunion. She actually told me she didn't know if she could tell everyone else her secret. I told her that it was not necessary. However, it was not long before she started dropping the "bombshell" on her friends.

It was summer and she and Ray were at the Jersey shore with friends. One night over dinner and drinks she told them about what had happened in her life back in 1963 and then what had happened a few months back. They were excited. Ray and Betsy were always the life of the party and the idea of her having an offspring was exciting. She and I would often talk while she was at the shore house and it wasn't long before her friends started getting on the phone with me and telling me stories. It was such a warm welcome. More than I could have hoped for.

One day during our conversation she told me she had told her brother. "You what?" I was shocked.

Much to her amazement, they were all thrilled. She told them with an introduction of "Remember when I took a leave of absence from flying back in the 60's ?."

Since Betsy had never had any other children, they thought it was wonderful. Many wanted to meet me. Her brother, sister-in-law, and nieces were ready to head to New Jersey when and if I arrived. So the planning of a face-to-face reunion began.

Betsy

Elizabeth Wilson Lockart was born in New Castle, Pennsylvania in October 1939 to William and Helen Lockhart. When Helen discovered she was pregnant, she also learned that she had an issue with her heart. But she didn't care, because she wanted to be a mother. And so her daughter was born. Sadly, three months later, Helen died due to complications with her heart. The pregnancy had been hard on her.

Betsy and her father moved in with her aunt, Peg. Aunt Peg asked that Betsy call her "Mother" and she spoiled the little girl to no end. William owned a vending company and traveled a lot, so Betsy was home with Aunt "Mother" Peg. When Betsy was about five,

her dad remarried and in a few years William and his
new wife, Shirley, had a son, a baby brother for Betsy:
William "Wink" Lockhart, Jr.

As Betsy tells it, she was boy crazy. She lists in her
notes to me that she spent her younger years going to
Lake Erie in the summers with her family, having
slumber parties, playing spin the bottle and driving her
parents nuts!

Betsy Lockhart in 1960 working as a Braniff flight attendent.

She admits that it
if it hadn't been for
her Uncle Coop, who
was president of the
local school board,
she might not have
graduated in 1957.
"Who would flunk
me? When he handed
my diploma he said 'I
never thought I would
see THIS day!'" she
recalled.

She moved to
Dallas, Texas, and became a flight attendant for Braniff
Airlines. In 1962, she and three other girlfriends planned
a trip to Hong Kong with a layover in Hawaii. On her
third day, while staying at the Hawaiian Village, she met
a good-looking surfer that folks called Ducky. (His real
name was Donald, but all cool surfers had a nickname.)

"Boy was he a big flirt," Betsy recalled. "But after our meeting, I said 'FORGET Hong Kong.' I was staying right there. He was such a doll and we spent three weeks together. We surfed (well, he surfed, I just sat on the board), we had dinner; we drank and had a really great time. I was crazy about him and other beach boys told me not to get too attached to Ducky, but I did. I cried when I had to leave. He gave me a lei and a big kiss and said to come back and visit." That was the last time she saw him or had contact with him.

A few weeks later back in Dallas, Betsy realized she was pregnant. She panicked. She kept on flying as long as she could and didn't tell a soul. "I finally told my roommates and they were very supportive and then I told my friend Mike. Mike was the one who found the place in Fort Worth. He made all the arrangements and I went there and I was once scared cookie."

While at Homestead, Betsy she said she met a few girls, but the fun-loving, life-of-the-party kept mostly to herself. "I never did get in touch with Ducky, I just didn't know what to say to him, and so I just did all myself," Betsy said.

The time drew near for Betsy to deliver. "After one false alarm, I went to the hospital in an ambulance and you arrived. I didn't want to know the sex, I just couldn't handle it. I went back home to Dallas to get on with my life, and decided not to look back," she said.

A few years later, Betsy's father was hit and killed while walking down the street, so she returned to Pennsylvania.

In 1982, she met Ray. As things got serious with
him, she mentioned that she had once had a baby and
given it up for adoption and then changed the subject.
He never raised the subject again and neither did Betsy.
Until the fateful day, THE LETTER arrived. Ray read it
and was very excited and thought it was wonderful. But
Betsy was too scared.

A few days later while talking to her sister-in-law Alix
(her brother Wink's wife), Alix said that a few weeks
ago one of Betsy's old flying buddies had called looking
for her. Betsy put two and two together and realized
that this "flying buddy" had to be connected to the
recent letter from a woman named Bonnie. Betsy told
Alix she was NOT to talk to anyone about her or give
out her information, that this woman she had spoken to
was a "nut." Alix thought it was strange that Betsy
reacted so strongly but agreed to follow her wishes.

Telling Mom and Dad the News

I knew then that my mom and dad must be told of
my search and finding my birthmother. I had not told
them that I was even searching. Not because I didn't
think they would be supportive but mostly because I
knew they would worry. They would be afraid of the
"what if's." I knew they would be afraid that I might get
hurt. But with the progression of the relationship
between me and Betsy, I had to fill them in.

I made a special trip home to see them. When I had
my mother alone I told her that I needed to tell her
something important and didn't want to upset her. I

started to tear up a little bit. Words got stuck in my throat. I just set there at the kitchen table.

Seeing my difficulty in finding words, she spoke first. Her first words were "What? Did you find your mama?"

I almost swallowed my tongue. This was unbelievable.

"YES--how on earth did you know?" I asked.

Mama replied "Because I can't think of anything else you might think would hurt me." She quickly assured me that it wouldn't hurt her. Then she continued to tell me how she was so happy for me and that how she had always wanted to locate her and "show me off". Mom was so grateful to this stranger and she wanted to let her know.

She said "you need to tell your daddy."

OH MY…I was terrified. Looking back, it is funny that I was so scared to tell such a gentle man. I think I was afraid that he would be hurt. We sat down to dinner and Mama kept looking at me,-wide eyed-, nodding, in Daddy's direction. Her body language screamed "Get on with it, girl!"

She broke the ice. "Ronna has something to tell you."

Thanks a lot, Mom!

Daddy looked at me with a raised brow and said "What is it babe?"

I started to cry and knew that if I didn't spit it out, his mind would travel down another road and he would be scared for me.

I don't recall exactly what I said but somehow I got through it. Mama chimed in a lot of "Isn't that great"…again screaming with her body language, "Evert, this is a good thing, support her!"

He patted me on the shoulder and said "If you are happy, I'm happy".

The next day I asked Mama what Daddy said when I was out of the room. He was awful quiet during my stuttering and stammering. She said that he just wondered why I hadn't told them I was searching. She assured him it was because I didn't want them to worry about me.

He said, "But what if she had gotten hurt and we wouldn't have known she needed us?" Oh, a father's love, so gentle and protecting.

Mama soon started gathering pictures of my life together so she could share them with Betsy. Next thing I knew, the two of them were corresponding via letters. Only a few letters, but enough for both of these women to thank the other for what they had done for the other. It showed me how remarkable both of these women were — and how fortunate I was to have both of them in my life.

Chapter 10
My Mother's Hands

New Jersey or Bust

Just as with the first email and the first phone conversation, the first meeting with Betsy brought extreme anxiety. I made arrangements and caught a plane to Philadelphia. Ray and Betsy would meet me there.

I didn't know how the three-hour flight would be for me. It was doubtful that I would sleep. I wouldn't be able to concentrate enough to read. There was no in-flight movie to distract me. I was probably just sit there and get very nervous. But the solution was sitting right next to me. I was sitting by an angel.

He didn't look much like an angel. About 5'6", 200 pounds and a sports writer for the Dallas Morning News. I sat by the window and he had the aisle seat. Casual conversation began and the common flight question was asked. "What are you headed to Philadelphia for?" I told him I was going to go meet my birthmother for the first time.

He was intrigued and started to ask lots of questions. He even asked if he could take notes. He said you never know when you will need an interesting story. I talked non-stop for the next three hours. Reliving the past few years actually calmed me. I cannot imagine what the plane ride would have been like if I had not been busy talking.

He had his photographer with him so I asked if he would take pictures of our reunion. Exiting the plane, I handed his photographer my camera. He started snapping away, capturing the escalator ride down, the first hug, the first tear. Pictures that are precious to me today. Pictures that might have been missed if it wasn't for the angel sitting in 10B.

Riding down the escalator, I spotted her standing out a ways. As I stepped off, she was closer and after walking a few feet, our eyes met. We didn't say anything at that moment. Didn't have to confirm who the other one was. We just embraced.

Betsy brought me

Our first moment at the Philadelphia International Airport.

flowers. We hugged so tight. Betsy and me. Ray and me. Then we sort of stood back and just looked at each other. Actually strangers, but also family.

I grabbed her hands. They were identical. It was remarkable. We shared the same hands. "We have the same hands, the exact same hands!" I shouted. Betsy just smiled.

We had planned each day of my stay. On the first day we would spend time together: just me, Betsy and Ray. The next day, a Friday, family and friends would meet for a feast...bringing out the fatted calf for the return of the child. In this case, the fatted calf was blue crab, shrimp, clams and several other items cooked in a manner like I never had experienced—it was delicious! There was lots of laughter, questions, pictures, and stories. It was quite overwhelming. I spent a lot of the time just sitting back "observing" — taking it all in. I

We are family!

quickly fell in love with my new uncle and his wife. Cousins and friends were so inviting. Betsy's two nieces, my cousins, Amanda and Suzanne didn't have cousins so they were excited to have a cousin on the Lockhart side of the family.

Ray, Wink, Alix, Amanda, Suzanne, Me & Betsy
(Top to Bottom, Left to Right)

Chapter 11
My Father's Legs

The Father's side

With my relationship with Betsy going strong, I wanted to call and introduce myself to "his" side of the family. I knew that he was deceased and Betsy had given me his name. She had told me that he was the

Ducky - 1957

cutest thing she had ever seen. She was actually on her way to Hong Kong with a few other flight attendants for a three week vacation. They had a one week layover in Hawaii. During this one week, she met him. Hong Kong would have to wait she cancelled the rest of her trip and stayed there with him. And, of course, when she got back to Texas, she realized that he would "be with her-in a sense" for the next nine months. I wanted to hear about his life. Betsy told me that he was a surfer and taught surfing at the hotel where she was staying. She said he was so cute she knew he must have a ton of girlfriends. But at that point she didn't care.

I wanted to get more information, so I began to search again. I knew his last name was Auld. I had his obituary which named a brother, Charles. So again, through the Internet, I found what I concluded was a cousin. I called and got a recording. "This is Audrey, Charlie and I aren't available. . ." I knew Charlie was my cousin and now I knew his wife's name. They stilled lived in Hawaii.

Ducky - age 4

This distance made calling Hawaii a challenge. In the mornings when I had all my "nerve," it was about 3 a.m. I didn't figure that would make a very good wake-up call or impression. And this was definitely news that needed to be introduced after morning coffee.

One Sunday afternoon, 5 p.m. Texas time and 1 p.m. Honolulu time, I dialed the number. Audrey answered. Somehow I got through the awkward introduction.

"Hello, my name is Ronna Quimby. I am an adopted child and I recently found my birthmother and it appears that Ducky was my birthfather." I do believe that I might have used other words and I know it took a while to get it all out, between the gulps and "uhs."

Audrey took it like a champ. And she didn't even appear to be shocked. She briefly told me that ol' Ducky was quite a party animal so she actually wasn't surprised. She told me that his sister-in-law, my aunt, would probably love to talk to me. She would find out and call me back. In a few minutes she called to let me know that Nonah was eager to talk to me and gave me her number. I called her immediately, told her who I was and what I believed to be the situation.

She said, "Do you have skinny legs?"

"Yes." I replied.

"Do you have green eyes?"

"Yes."

"Yep, you're an Auld," she confirmed.

Wow, was that all it took for them to believe the story? Evidently so. Of course as soon as I saw a picture of Ducky's legs and realized how much they looked like mine, I understood. She began to tell me about Ducky, about his short life.

Lavina with Baby
My Maternal Grandmother

A week or so later, Charlie (Nonah's) son called me. My cousin.

He told me how his "Uncle Ducky" was the life of the party and his memories of him were all about having fun and living life on the edge. He said that it was almost to the point that when he died at age 45, the sadness was less because all knew that he had squeezed every bit of fun out of life. His name was actually Donald but as a surfer, developed the name Ducky. His father, Charles, was called Chicken.

Ducky - June 1952
Graduation from Kamehameda

I told Charlie that I knew Betsy was not shy and not one to turn down a party as well, so they were perfectly matched. He asked me if I had a "wild side." I told him no not really and that I was raised very differently—a conservative-Baptist-upbringing. He said for me not to fear too much about it because my grandfather—Ducky's dad—was a deacon in the oldest church in Hilo, Hawaii. He wanted me to make sure I told my parents about that.

So I did . . . I told my parents and then sent out an email to update all of those who were tracking this story.

Shortly my phone rang. It was Rebekah, the one who had forced me to press SEND in the first place.

She said, "You are not going to believe this. My father was the pastor of that church in Hilo. I called him and asked him if he remembered a family named *Auld.* He said, 'Yeah, Chicken.' "

Holy shit! How could this be? The world just seemed a whole lot smaller. Who could have dreamed that I would work in Arlington, Texas, with a girl whose dad was a pastor in a church in Hawaii where my grandfather was a deacon? This is one of those stories you hear on "Oprah."

Hawaii

Now there could have been worse places I would have to visit on this quest. But if it was Hawaii, then Hawaii it must be…Yee Haw—ALOHA!!!!

Alix & Me

It was May 2004. I was now 41 and had reservations for Hawaii. I asked Betsy if she wanted to accompany me and she declined, saying that it would be to "weird." So I asked my new Aunt Alix. Alix was married to Betsy's brother, Wink (William). She was thrilled. Alix is what I would call a free spirit. Fun, carefree, and we hit it off back in New Jersey when I visited.

Our plan was to go to Honolulu and stay a few days and then head to the Big Island to Kona where my new Aunt Nonah and her son, my cousin and brother to Charlie, Castle, lived. We really enjoyed our first few days in Waikii and then the day came to head to Kona. Castle's wife was going to pick us up and take us to our hotel and we would plan out the next couple of days.

When Ku'ulani picked us up, it was so natural, just

Julie & Me

were never any minutes of awkwardness or uneasiness. It was almost familiar.

We soon learned that we shared the same passion for rodeo. Billy is a retired bull rider and bareback rider and now a rodeo announcer. Ku'ulani and Castle and especially their son, Sam, were heavily evolved in rodeo. Matter of fact, they lived not to far from the Parker Ranch- one of the largest ranches in the world. Who would imagine that being a rodeo enthusiast would be something that I would share with my Hawaiian relatives?

Castle, me and the chicken.

We were dropped off at the hotel with instructions that she would be back in a couple of hours to pick us up. We would go to Nonah's for dinner.

Arriving at Nonah's, I met her, my new cousin and his two sons. Again, the evening was so familiar. We made leis, looked at pictures and got acquainted.

Nonah told me that while I was in Honolulu, I needed to look up Julie. Julie was Ducky's first cousin and they were inseparable as children and teens. She said she would make an "introductory" call and I could call her after that. We'll see....

After our wonderful stay in Kona we headed back to Oahu. Alix had to leave and I still had three more days left to enjoy this paradise. During my quiet days, I decided to call Julie.

She appeared thrilled to hear from me. Julie wanted to meet for breakfast the next day. I agreed.

I pulled up at the little diner to meet her and her husband the next morning. Again, I was welcomed with open arms. Julie cried and held on to me and said she was so glad to have a part of Ducky back. After breakfast, she and I went on a little tour of her world. We went to the school where she was principal. She even offered me a job (and I will say, if I hadn't had my family waiting back in Texas, I think I might have stayed at least one quarter—hell, it is HAWAII!!!)

She shared photos, stories, hugs, tears and then of course, we had to have our good-byes. Luckily we still keep in touch...I am her little piece of Ducky.

I had mentioned that I had Betsy's hands. Well, Nonah was right in asking about my skinny legs because in one photo of Ducky, it is almost like someone cropped in MY legs for his...the same knees, the same ankles . . .

Wow . . . I finally looked like someone.

Donald "Ducky" Auld

Ducky was born in Hilo, Hawaii to Charles and Lavina Auld on February 15, 1934. When Ducky was younger than three years old, his mother left, leaving Charles to care for his two sons: Ducky and his older brother Charlie. Charles worked for the government as a port inspector. When Ducky was seven, his dad remarried and for the remainder of his life, he considered his step mother, Molly, as his mother. Charles and Molly were always there when Ducky had a need . . . be it an extra few dollars or a place to stay.

Ducky was a natural musician. When he picked up any instrument, it was a matter of time before he was playing a tune. He was the life of the party. He considered himself quite the singer. (wonder if HE could sing "All of Me" in the key of F?) His cousin Julie only remarked "well, HE thought he could sing."

FRI MAR 3 0 1979 SB M
Donald Auld

Donald U. "Ducky" Auld, 45, of 1634 Makiki St., a state pilot boat operator and former beach boy, died Tuesday in Kaiser Hospital.

Funeral services will be held at 10 a.m. Monday on the beach at the Elks Club. The ashes will be scattered at sea.

The family requests that flowers be omitted and that aloha attire be worn. Contributions may be made to Elks Lodge 616.

Mr. Auld was born in Hilo.

He is survived by his wife, Margaret; his father, Charles Auld; his stepmother, Molly, of Hilo; his mother, Lavina Kinsley of Texas, and a brother, Charles Jr. of Kaneohe.

When Ducky was ready to enter the 7th grade he was admitted to private military school in Oahu, Kamehameha School. This was a highly prestigious school for Hawaiian children founded by Princess Bernice Pauahi Bishop. He attended the Kapalama campus in Oahu. After graduation, he stayed in Honolulu and began teaching tourist to surf. He was one of Hawaii's beach boys. He worked at the Hilton Hawaiian Village

Charles Auld, Sr.
My Maternal Grandfather

teaching surfing and in 1962, met one Elizabeth Lockhart.

Later in his life he worked as a tug boat captain. He was a true ladies man but when he was forty, he married Margaret. Margaret was a school counselor who worked doing testing for special needs students.

In just a few short years after his marriage, he was diagnosed with cancer. His nephews report that he was in tremendous pain for a year but always kept the party going. His cousin Julie said that during the last year of his life Ducky "made the rounds" to visit family, to say his last good-byes. She fondly recalls him saying "Hey cuz, I sure had a good life." No one disagreed. All the family agreed that in his 44 years, he lived a lifetime. He died on March 3, 1979, forty days shy of his 45th birthday. His funeral service was held at the beach, ashes were cast upon the water off the Waikiki beach. Several tug boats were in the bay and circled the area where the ashes were scattered, blowing their horns, stirring up the water and creating a beautiful spray of water. A fitting good-bye to a beach boy who loved the Island and the water.

Chapter 12
Answers and Understanding

Homestead has an on-line "community" where folks who are searching-birthchildren and birth mothers alike get together and share thoughts, ideas, stories…the good, the bad and the ugly. I was asked to join this group.

Actually it was five years after I was re-united with Betsy, but I still joined the group. I would read about people's searches, their feelings, fears, and anxiety. I tried so hard to remember what it was like when I didn't know…..when I was searching….Googling the Internet every day…fearful and anxious of what was out there. Wondering when would I find the answers I was seeking. How would I find them? And now, here I was years later with so many answers. I had come full circle. Were my answers what I had expecting? Were the blanks filled in correctly? Was it enough? Had it changed me?

It is sort of like waiting for something for such a long time, wanting it soooo long that when you finally, finally, get it, the response is more like "hmmmm, yep, there it is." In the movie *Vacation* with Chevy Chase, he is so excited that his family is going to see the Grand Canyon . . . they actually go miles out of their way to see it. They face all sorts of detours, struggles and roadblocks.

They talk it up about how wonderful it will be when they get there and then when they pull up they rush out of the car, full of excitement and stand at the edge for a few minutes. Nod their heads, survey the view, and sort of "hmmm". "hmmmm"—translation: "Yep, there it is." They get back in the car and they move on.

That is a fairly close analogy of my experience. I searched for years, thought about searching, talked about the excitement for even longer. I faced detours, struggles, roadblocks, but I finally found what I was searching. I'm very glad that I did but still my overall view is sort of an "hmmmm." None of the people, whose lives have changed because of my search, can change the fact that they have been discovered. I believe that none of them would want to go back to "not knowing." We love each other. They are my family. And at this point, really not even different from the relationship I have with my other relatives (my adopted relatives).

I firmly believe that many times adoptees make a rush decision to find their answers before taking the time to know what the real questions may be. The question is not just "who are my birthparents?" It is a question of "who am I?" One has to find who they are inside. Realize that they are significant in this world—even without answers of birth history. Many times, we set out on life's journeys with expectations that often lead to heartache. We look outward for fulfillment. "I will feel whole when I find my birthmother." "I will feel whole when I find out why she gave me away." Are those expectations and conclusions ones that will <u>really</u> make us whole?

It is understandable that all this "wholeness" may not happen all at once and actually when you think you are whole and you start on the journey, you find out you still have a lot to learn about yourself. Not just because of the "filling in the blanks," but also because you realize that you are not about what is missing.

I firmly believe and encourage all those who seek answers to take a look at their expectations. IS this about highlighting your life or is it about giving you a life. It cannot be about giving you a life. You are significant. You, we, are more than the answers.

A Real Loss

In October 2005 and October 2006, I lost my father and mother-Evert and Frances. Daddy was in a nursing home for the last 60 days of his life. After years of heart disease, his heart just gave out. Less than a year later, my mother passed away. Ten days prior, she had been diagnosed with liver cancer. I had always wondered when my parents died would I need my birthmother to fill the void? Being an only child, I would be all alone without a connection. They have now been gone a few years. I miss them terribly. The void their passing left in my heart is not filled by my relationship with Betsy. It is filled by the memories of a wonderful life. I know that I am so very lucky. Their passing has not changed my relationship with Betsy or her family. They are family and I love and enjoy them.

In my world, Betsy is not my mother as I define it, nor will she ever fill the void left by my mother. Betsy fills a part of my heart that is only for her. Betsy is a wonderful, special woman who, when faced with a difficult decision, gave me a life so special that I will never be able to repay her. I was raised by a mother and father who thought I hung the moon. They provided me with all I ever needed: love, security, guidance, and laughter. Because of them, I have a strong sense of self, nature, and mankind. I notice the colors of the sunset, the butterflies in the garden, the morning dew on the grass, and all of God's wonderful creatures.

Relating to Betsy was new territory. How would you define this relationship? I had a mother...even though she was gone now. I try and call Betsy as often as possible, but that good intent often falls by the wayside. It can sometimes be several weeks in between our conversations. She is always so kind on the phone and thanks me for calling and that it is good to hear from me but I often wonder if it all really matters. Again, is it just an obligation on both our parts to keep in touch? Don't get me wrong, I think we are both thankful for the opportunity to know each other. But when you really think about it, the goal of adoption is to sever ties with the biological mother. But this was the actual woman who gave birth to me, the one who met the definition of *mother* by most. And I'm sure it was difficult for her as well — 39 years later a stranger whom you had worked so hard to put in your past, to keep out of your thoughts, a person whose existence had brought you fear, sadness, guilt, shame.

She had no other children, so she had no experience on how to "relate" to a child, to be a *mother.* And honestly, she didn't want to be a mother....so the struggle began. I wonder if she would have had the experience of being a parent, if that would change how she and I interact. Were we now obligated to keep a relationship going?

Alix and Wink are great. I really feel close to them. The have been so generous with gifts, greeting cards, calls, and love. I think maybe because I knew how to relate to an aunt and uncle (because I HAD aunts and uncles) it was really easy to define our relationship. You-aunt, me-niece.

I love Betsy. Our interaction is more like close family friends than what we really are, which is mother and daughter. It even feels strange calling us mother and daughter. Maybe that is because I was able to share a fulfilling relationship with my mother Frances and even after the void of her death, I don't need someone else to step in and be a mother to me.

When I read the posts made on the Homestead Maternity Home Yahoo Group, I wonder if those searching will experience the same kind of experience when they find their loved ones. It is extremely difficult for me to think back and experience the feelings of longing that I did before I found Betsy. The "somewhere out there" is no longer a mystery.

Sharing My life

In 2005, Billy and I married. Billy is a wonderful writer and a driving force in my journey to find and record my search. He brought me strength and also brought me two wonderful daughters. Cindy (22) and Stacy (12) are my "bonus" daughters. We don't use the word "step-daughter" or "step-mother" because they are more than that. They are a bonus to my wonderful relationship. They are strong, unique, healthy individuals. They are a joy.

I take being part of their lives very seriously. Their parents have done a wonderful job and I want to be a positive influence as well. I want to give them a strong sense of self, remind them to notice the colors of the sunset, the flowers in the fields. I was never fortunate to have children of my own but being blessed with bonus

children is just that, a blessing. I had the best mother role model and I hope to pass along what I can.

I know that being a bonus mom differs from being an adoptive mother but there are some similarities. We both are given an opportunity to influence children who are not born to us. It is like a special friendship and almost reminds me of my relationship with Betsy. Cindy and Stacy don't *need* a mother, they have a mother. But I do have a special role to play in their lives. I try my hardest to be what they need. I am significant in their world.

Overview - A Significant Life

I am Ronna Quimby Huckaby. I am an adopted child. I am loved by two mothers. One who gave birth to me and the one who made my life so fulfilling.

In the remake of the movie *Cape Fear*, the daughter, Danielle, speaks the following line at the end of the movie: *if you hold on to the past you die a little each day and for myself I want to live.* I think it is important that we face the past but we do not have to hold on to it. We must take from it what we need.

Remember, we must look at the questions we are asking and make sure that they are the questions that we want answered. The questions asked may be *Why was I put up for adoption?* When we are <u>really</u> feeling unworthy or less than and we want to ask *What is wrong with me?* Of course, we know that nothing is wrong with us. We are significant. However, we must come to the understanding of our issues as we work to feel whole and complete.

I do not feel that I am missing anything in my search for answers. Yet so many times, I felt that the answers were still somewhere out there. I have asked "what is wrong with me?" and I had to realize that I was significant: Significant, regardless of feeling sometimes "less than", significant, regardless of realizing my many mistakes, significant, regardless of the fact that I was adopted. I just had to decided if the answers that I was seeking were going to define my life or if they would only highlight a life already defined— defined by a loving home, a loving family and a bright future.

I have come to realize that the answers to my many questions have been with me all along.

It took some time. It took some looking. I just had to look a little deeper to realize it. I had to allow myself to experience *being* an adopted child and what that means to me — all the emotions as painful or as joyous as they might be. I could not be afraid of what I would find when I looked deeper. I could not be afraid of what I would not find when I looked deeper. I had to discover that the answers to the question would not make me whole. Adopted children are not "less than." We are already whole; we are not just a piece of a scattered life.

We are all important creatures on this earth. We seek love and understanding. We deserve love and understanding. We must realize that both of these start inside. We must make this discovery and not look to the external things for our completion. Others will not make us whole, we cannot fill holes with outside things.

Waiting for others or answers to make us complete will never happen. Easier said than done but this is the truth. We are not a sum of our external variables; we are actors in our story, not re-actors in the story of others. Fulfillment of self comes from within. We are the sum of our "self"--the internal self, the true face in the mirror.

I survived the feelings of hurt, anger, rejection, and came out on the other side whole. It was not always an easy journey. It was not always a pleasant journey but it was worth the trip. Coming to know one's self can be scary. There were times I didn't know if I would make it to the end and believe that I was not what others thought. I was just me. And looking back, I am who I am today because of the path I have walked--all the turns and miles have brought me to where I am today. I like today.

This is MY experience and understanding of adoption. I do not think that it is so unique. I hope that for others who are adopted, finding some similarities can assist in the journey thorough life as an adopted child.

What are the questions that we ask? What are the answers we seek? Where are we seeking to find the answers? Maybe realizing that the experience of finding a birthparent, or some "magical" answers aren't such a big deal as we might anticipate.

We must first realize that the "somewhere out there" is not "out there". It is really just a place in our heart. That is the place where we can make our dreams come true....within is where you will find the true answers.

The Quimby Family - Evert is standing behind his mother.

College Graduation

Cousins
Ronna
Doria
Kyla

The Johnson Sisters - Peb, Frances and Pauline

Cousins
Kevin
Ronna
Riley

Singing while standing on an ice chest seems to be hereditary.

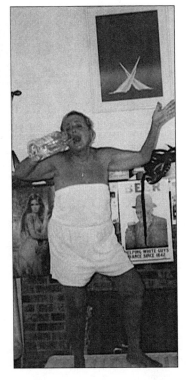

Billy & Ronna

**Beautiful Bonus Daughters
Stacy & Cindy**

About the Author

She lived an idyllic life in small town Texas and Ronna Quimby Huckaby never lacked for love. She lived a life that could have been a 1950s television show. Bowie, Texas, much like Mayberry and a mother reminiscent of June Cleaver, was the setting for Ronna's first eighteen years.

Ronna grew up knowing she was adopted, but always had the thought in the back of mind as to why she was given up for adoption and who were her birth parents. Despite the doubts and thoughts she lived a happy and normal life. She was popular in school, active in her community and respected by her peers.

Following graduation from high school Ronna earned a bachelor's degree at and a Masters of Education in counseling from the University of North Texas. She is a licensed professional counselor and board approved counselor supervisor. Ronna has worked in the nonprofit field 21 years, primarily with agencies that dealt with domestic violence, homelessness, and substance abuse.

Ronna is currently chief operation officer of Recovery Resource Council in Fort Worth, Texas. She also serves on the board of the Texas chapter of the Association of Substance Abuse Programs. She lives in Walnut Springs, Texas with her husband Billy, 3 dogs-Sadie, Tucker, and Gus and cat, Nabor. She also enjoys sharing the lives of her bonus daughters, Cindy and Stacy.

Photo by Lauren Deen - www.ldeenphotography.com

Searching & Registry Websites
Below is a list of useful websites for adoptees and birthfamilies

Texas Coalition for Adoption Resources and Education
www.txcare.org

Part of Ancestry.com
www.rootsweb.com

Adoption Registry
Free service provided by TxCare
www.adoptionregistry.us

Adoption Registry Connect
A worldwide adoptee and birth parent search registry.
www.adopteeconnect.com

FindMe
Free adoption registry database.
www.findme.org

The Adoption Database
www.adoptiondatabase.org

Adoption Search Registry
Register your adoption search.
www.adoptionsearchbureau.com

Adoption Search – Birthmother and Adoptee Reunion
www.adopting.org

For Texas Adoptions
www.dshs.state.tx.us

LaVergne, TN USA
05 March 2011
218928LV00001B/6/P